Adventure
in
Prolog

Dennis Merritt

Adventure in Prolog — Copyright 2017 Dennis Merritt

Preface

I was working for an aerospace company in the 1970s when someone got a copy of the original Adventure game (a simulated world the player explores, at that time purely text-based, with natural language) and installed it on our mainframe computer. For the next month my lunch hours, evenings and weekends, as well as normal work hours, were consumed with fighting the fierce green dragon and escaping from the twisty little passages. Finally, with a few hints about the plover's egg and dynamite, I had proudly earned all the points in the game.

My elation turned to terror as I realized it was time for my performance review. My boss was a stern man, who was more comfortable with machines than people. He opened up a large computer printout containing a log of the hours each of his programmers spent on the mainframe computer. He said he noticed that recently I had been working evenings and weekends and that he admired that type of dedication in his employees. He gave me the maximum raise and told me to keep up the good work.

Ever since I've had a warm spot in my heart for adventure games.

Years later, when I got my first home computer, I immediately started to write my own adventure game in 'C'. First came the tools, a simple dynamic database to keep track of the game state, and pattern matching functions to search that database. Then came a natural language parser for the front end. Functions implemented the various rules of the game.

At around the same time I joined the Boston Computer Society and attended a lecture of the newly formed Artificial Intelligence group. The lecture was about Prolog. I was amazed—here was a language that included all of the tools needed for building adventure games and more.

It had a much richer dynamic database and more powerful pattern matcher than the one I had written, plus its syntax was rules, which are much more natural for coding the specification of the game. It had a built-in search engine and, to top it all off, had tools for natural language processing.

I learned Prolog from the classic Clocksin and Mellish text and started writing adventure games anew.

I went on to use Prolog for a number of expert system applications at my then current job, including a mainframe database performance tuning system and installation expert. This got others interested in the language and I began teaching it as well.

While the applications we were using Prolog for were serious and performed a key role in improving technical support for the growing company, I still found the adventure game to be an excellent showcase for teaching the language.

This book is the result of that work. It takes a pragmatic, rather than theoretical, approach to the language and is designed for programmers interested in adding this powerful language to their bag of tools.

I offer my thanks to Will Crowther and Don Woods for writing the first (and in my opinion still the best) adventure game and to the Boston Computer Society for testing the ideas in the book. Thanks also to Ray Reeves, who speaks fluent Prolog, and Nancy Wilson, who speaks fluent English, for their careful reading of the text.

Dennis Merritt

Stow, Massachusetts, April 1996

Table of Contents

1- Getting Started

Prolog stands for PROgramming in LOGic. It was developed from a foundation of logical theorem proving and originally used for research in natural language processing. Although its popularity has sprung up mainly in the artificial intelligence (AI) community, where it has been used for applications such as expert systems, natural language, and intelligent databases, it is also useful for more conventional types of applications. It allows for more rapid development and prototyping than most languages because it is semantically close to the logical specification of a program. As such, it approaches the ideal of executable program specifications.

Programming in Prolog is significantly different from conventional procedural programming and requires a readjustment in the way one thinks about programming. Logical relationships are asserted, and Prolog is used to determine whether or not certain statements are true, and if true, what variable bindings make them true. This leads to a very declarative style of programming.

While Prolog is a fascinating language from a purely theoretical viewpoint, this book will stress Prolog as a practical programming language, well suited for full application development.

Much of the book will be built around the writing of a short adventure game. The adventure game is a good example since it contains mundane programming constructs, symbolic reasoning, natural language, database, and logic.

Through exercises you will also build a simple expert system, an intelligent genealogical database, and a mundane customer order entry application.

You should create a source file for the game, and enter the examples from the book as you go. You should also create source files for the other three programs covered in the exercises. Sample source code for each of the programs is included in the appendix.

The adventure game is called Nani Search. Your persona as the adventurer is that of a three year old girl. The lost treasure with magical powers is your nani (security blanket). The terrifying obstacle between you and success is a dark room. It is getting late and you're tired, but you can't go to sleep without your nani. Your mission is to find the nani.

Nani Search is composed of

- A read and execute command loop
- A natural language input parser
- A database describing the current environment
- Commands that manipulate the environment
- Puzzles that must be solve

You control the game by using simple English commands (at the angle bracket (>) prompt) expressing the action you wish to take. You can go to other rooms, look at your surroundings, look in things, take things, drop things, eat things, inventory the things you have, and turn things on and off.

Figure 1.1 shows a run of a completed version of Nani Search. As you develop your own version you can of course change the game to reflect your own ideas of adventure.

The game will be implemented from the bottom up, because that fits better with the order in which the topics will be introduced. Prolog is equally adept at supporting top-down or inside-out program development.

A Prolog program exists in the listener's workspace as a collection of small modular units, called **predicates**. They are similar to subroutines in conventional languages, but on a smaller scale.

The predicates can be added and tested separately in a Prolog program, which makes it possible to incrementally develop the applications described in the book. Each chapter will call for the addition of more and more predicates to the game. Similarly, the exercises will ask you to add predicates to each of the other applications.

We will start with the Nani Search database and quickly move into the commands that examine that database. Then we will implement the commands that manipulate the database.

Along the way there will be diversions where the same commands are rewritten using a different approach for comparison. Occasionally a topic will be covered that is critical to Prolog but has little application in Nani Search.

One of the final tasks will be putting together the top-level command processor. We will finish with the natural language interface.

```
You are in the kitchen.
You can see: apple, table, broccoli
You can go to: cellar, office, dining room

> go to the cellar

You can't go to the cellar because it's dark in the
cellar, and you're afraid of the dark.

> turn on the light

You can't reach the switch and there's nothing to
stand on.

> go to the office

You are in the office.
You can see the following things: desk
You can go to the following rooms: hall, kitchen

> open desk

The desk contains:
   flashlight
   crackers

> take the flashlight

You now have the flashlight
```

```
> kitchen

You are in the kitchen

> turn on the light

flashlight turned on.
...
```

Figure 1.1. A sample run of Nani Search

The goal of this book is to make you feel comfortable with

- The Prolog database of facts and rules
- The built-in theorem prover that allows Prolog to answer questions about the database (backtracking search)
- How logical variables are used (They are different from the variables in most languages.)
- Unification, the built in pattern matcher
- Extra-logical features (like read and write that make the language practical)
- How to control Prolog's execution behavior

Jumping In

As with any language, the best way to learn Prolog is to use it. This book is designed to be used with a Prolog listener, and will guide you through the building of four applications.

- Adventure game
- Intelligent genealogical database
- Expert system
- Customer order entry business application

The adventure game will be covered in detail in the main body of the text, and the others you will build yourself based on the exercises at the end of each chapter.

There will be two types of example code throughout the book. One is code, meant to be entered in a source file, and the other is interactions with the listener. The listener interactions are distinguished by the presence of the question mark and dash (?-) listener prompt.

Here is a two-line program, meant to help you learn the mechanics of the editor and your listener.

```
mortal(X) :- person(X).

person(socrates).
```

Figure out how to create and edit a source code file for your Prolog implementation.

[Amzi Prolog – In the Amzi! Eclipse IDE, first create a project for your source files. Select FilelNewlProject on the main menu, then click on 'Prolog' and 'Project', and enter the name of your project, 'adventure'. Next, create a new source file. Select FilelNewlFile, and enter the name of your file, 'mortal.pro'. Enter the program in the edit window, paying careful attention to upper and lowercase letters and punctuation. Then select FilelSave from the menu.]

Then figure out how to consult that file into the Prolog listener to run it.

[Amzi Prolog – Start the Prolog listener by selecting the file you just created and using a right mouse click select RunlRunAsl Interpreted Project.]

You should see the typical listener prompt.

```
?-
```

Entering the source code in the Listener is called consulting. You can also consult a Prolog source file directly from the listener prompt like this.

```
?- consult(mortal).
yes
```

See the documentation and/or online help for details for your Prolog.

In all the listener examples in this book, you enter the text after the prompt (?-), the rest is provided by Prolog. When working with Prolog, it is important to remember to include the final period and to press the 'return' key. If you forget the period (and you probably will), you can enter it on the next line with a 'return.'

Once you've loaded the program, try the following Prolog queries.

```
?- mortal(socrates).
yes
?- mortal(X).
X = socrates.
```

Now let's change the program. Go back to the edit window and add the line

```
person(plato).
```

after the person(socrates) line.

If you 'consult' your file again, you will have two copies of your predicates in the listener. To replace the old version in the listener, select Listener/Reconsult, or simply press the toolbar button with the letters 'Re' to reconsult the last file consulted. You can also reconsult directly from the listener.

```
?- reconsult(mortal).
yes
```

And test it.

```
?- mortal(plato).
yes
```

One more test. Enter this query in the listener.

```
?- write('Hello World').
Hello World
yes
```

You are now ready to learn Prolog.

Logic Programming

Let's look at the simple example in more detail. In classical logic we might say "All people are mortal," or, rephrased for Prolog, "For all X, X is mortal if X is a person."

```
mortal(X) :- person(X).
```

Similarly, we can assert the simple fact that Socrates is a person.

```
person(socrates).
```

From these two logical assertions, Prolog can now prove whether or not Socrates is mortal.

```
?- mortal(socrates).
```

The listener responds

```
yes
```

We could also ask "Who is mortal?" like this

```
?- mortal(X).
```

and receive the response

```
X = socrates
```

This declarative style of programming is one of Prolog's major strengths. It leads to code that is easier to write and easier to maintain. For the most part, the programmer is freed from having to worry about control structures and transfer of control mechanisms. This is done automatically by Prolog.

By itself, however, a logical theorem prover is not a practical programming tool. A programmer needs to do things that have nothing to do with logic, such as read and write terms. A programmer also needs to manipulate the built-in control structure of Prolog in order for the program to execute as desired.

The following example illustrates a Prolog program that prints a report of all the known mortals. It is a mixture of pure logic from before, extra-logical I/O, and forced control of the Prolog execution behavior. The example is illustrative only, and the concepts involved will be explained in later chapters.

First add some more philosophers to the 'mortal' source in order to make the report more interesting. Place them after 'person(plato).'

```
person(zeno).
person(aristotle).
```

Next add the report-writing code, again being careful with punctuation and upper- and lowercase. Note that the format of this program is the same as that used for the logical assertions.

```
mortal_report:-
    write('Known mortals are:'),nl,
    mortal(X),
    write(X),nl,
    fail.
```

Figure 1.2 contains the full program, with some optional comments, indicated by the percent sign (%) at the beginning of a line. Load the program in the listener and try it. Note that the syntax of calling the report code is the same as the syntax used for posing the purely logical queries.

```
?- mortal_report.
Known mortals are:
socrates
plato
aristotle
no
```

The final 'no' is from Prolog, and will be explained later.

```
% This is the syntax for comments.
% MORTAL - The first illustrative Prolog program

mortal(X) :- person(X).

person(socrates).
person(plato).
person(aristotle).

mortal_report:-
```

```
write('Known mortals are:'),nl,
mortal(X),
write(X),nl,
fail.
```
Figure 1.2. Sample program

You should now be able to create and edit source files for Prolog, and be able to load and use them from a Prolog listener.

You have had your first glimpse of Prolog and should understand that it is fundamentally different from most languages, but can be used to accomplish the same goals and more.

Jargon

With any field of knowledge, the critical concepts of the field are embedded in the definitions of its technical terms. Prolog is no exception. When you understand terms such as **predicate**, **clause**, **backtracking**, and **unification** you will have a good grasp of Prolog. This section defines the terms used to describe Prolog programs, such as predicate and clause. Execution-related terms, such as backtracking and unification will be introduced as needed throughout the rest of the text.

Prolog jargon is a mixture of programming terms, database terms, and logic terms. You have probably heard most of the terms before, but in Prolog they don't necessarily mean what you think they mean.

In Prolog the normally clear distinction between data and procedure becomes blurred. This is evident in the vocabulary of Prolog. Almost every concept in Prolog can be referred to by synonymous terms. One of the terms has a procedural flavor, and the other a data flavor.

We can illustrate this at the highest level. A Prolog **program** is a Prolog database. As we introduce the vocabulary of Prolog, synonyms (from Prolog or other computer science areas) for a term will follow in parentheses. For example, at the highest level we have a Prolog program (database).

The Prolog program is composed of **predicates** (procedures, record types, relations). Each is defined by its name and a number called arity. The arity is the fixed number of arguments (attributes, fields) the predicate has. Two predicates with the same name and different arity are considered to be different predicates.

In our sample program we saw three examples of predicates. They are: person/1, mortal_report/0, and mortal/1. Each of these three predicates has a distinctly different flavor.

person/1	Looks like multiple data records with one data field for each.
mortal_report/0	Looks like a procedure with no arguments.
mortal/1	A logical assertion or rule that is somewhere in between data and procedure.

Each predicate in a program is defined by the existence of one or more clauses in the database. In the example program, the predicate person/1 has four clauses. The other predicates have only one clause.

A clause can be either a **fact** or a **rule**. The three clauses of the person/1 predicate are all facts. The single clauses of mortal_report/0 and mortal/1 are both rules.

2- Facts

This chapter describes the basic Prolog facts. They are the simplest form of Prolog predicates, and are similar to records in a relational database. As we will see in the next chapter they can be queried as a database.

The syntax for a fact is

```
pred(arg1, arg2, ...  argN).
```
Where

pred	The name of the predicate
arg1, arg2, ... argN	The arguments
N	The arity (number of arguments)
.	The period syntactic end of all Prolog clauses

A predicate of arity 0 is simply

```
pred.
```
The arguments can be any legal Prolog term. The basic Prolog terms are

integer	A positive or negative number whose absolute value is less than some implementation-specific power of 2
atom	A text constant beginning with a lowercase letter
variable	Begins with an uppercase letter or underscore (_)
structure	Complex terms, which will be covered in chapter 9

Various Prolog implementations enhance this basic list with other data types, such as floating point numbers, or strings.

The Prolog character set is made up of

- Uppercase letters, A-Z
- Lowercase letters, a-z
- Digits, 0-9
- Symbols, + - * / \ ^ , . ~ : . ? @ # $ &

Integers are made from digits. Other numerical types are allowed in some Prolog implementations.

Atoms are usually made from letters and digits with the first character being a lowercase letter, such as

```
hello
twoWordsTogether
x14
```

For readability, the underscore (_), but not the hyphen (-), can be used as a separator in longer names. So the following are legal.

```
a_long_atom_name
z_23
```

The following are not legal atoms.

```
no-embedded-hyphens
123nodigitsatbeginning
_nounderscorefirst
Nocapsfirst
```

Use single quotes to make any character combination a legal atom as follows.

```
'this-hyphen-is-ok'
'UpperCase'
'embedded blanks'
```

Do not use double quotes ("") to build atoms. This is a special syntax that causes the character string to be treated as a list of ASCII character codes.

Atoms can also be legally made from symbols, as follows.

```
-->
```

```
++
```

Variables are similar to atoms, but are distinguished by beginning
with either an uppercase letter or the underscore (_).

```
X
Input_List
_4th_argument
Z56
```

Using these building blocks, we can start to code facts. The
predicate name follows the rules for atoms. The arguments can be
any Prolog terms.

Facts are often used to store the data a program is using. For
example, a business application might have customer/3.

```
customer('John Jones', boston,
good_credit).
customer('Sally Smith', chicago,
good_credit).
```

The single quotes are needed around the names because they begin
with uppercase letters and because they have embedded blanks.

Another example is a windowing system that uses facts to store
data about the various windows. In this example the arguments
give the window name and coordinates of the upper left and lower
right corners.

```
window(main, 2, 2, 20, 72).
window(errors, 15, 40, 20, 78).
```

A medical diagnostic expert system might have disease/2.

```
disease(plague, infectious).
```

A Prolog listener provides the means for recording facts and rules
in the dynamic database, as well as the means to query (call) them.
The database is updated by 'consult'ing or 'reconsult'ing program
source. Predicates can also be typed directly into the listener, but
they are not saved between sessions.

Nani Search

We will now begin to develop Nani Search by defining the basic facts that are meaningful for the game. These include

- The rooms and their connections
- The things and their locations
- The properties of various things
- Where the player is at the beginning of the game

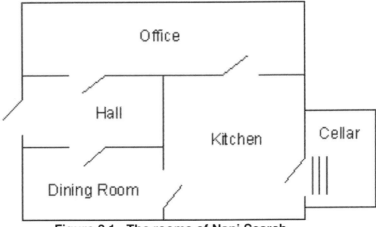

Figure 2.1. The rooms of Nani Search

Open a new source file and save it as 'myadven.pro', or whatever name you feel is appropriate. You will make your changes to the program in that source file. (A completed version of nanisrch.pro is in the Prolog samples directory, PROSAMP.)

First we define the rooms with the predicate room/1, which has five clauses, all of which are facts. They are based on the game map in figure 2.1.

```
room(kitchen).
room(office).
room(hall).
room('dining room').
room(cellar).
```

We define the locations of things with a two-argument predicate location/2. The first argument will mean the thing and the second will mean its location. To begin with, we will add the following things.

```
location(desk, office).
location(apple, kitchen).
location(flashlight, desk).
location('washing machine', cellar).
location(nani, 'washing machine').
location(broccoli, kitchen).
location(crackers, kitchen).
location(computer, office).
```

The symbols we have chosen, such as kitchen and desk have meaning to us, but none to Prolog. The relationship between the arguments should also accurately reflect our meaning.

For example, the meaning we attach to location/2 is "The first argument is located in the second argument." Fortunately Prolog considers location(sink, kitchen) and location(kitchen, sink) to be different. Therefore, as long as we are consistent in our use of arguments, we can accurately represent our meaning and avoid the potentially ambiguous interpretation of the kitchen being in the sink.

We are not as lucky when we try to represent the connections between rooms. Let's start, however, with door/2, which will contain facts such as

```
door(office, hall).
```

We would like this to mean "There is a connection from the office to the hall, or from the hall to the office."

Unfortunately, Prolog considers door(office, hall) to be different from door(hall, office). If we want to accurately represent a two-way connection, we would have to define door/2 twice for each connection.

```
door(office, hall).
door(hall, office).
```

The strictness about order serves our purpose well for location, but it creates this problem for connections between rooms. If the office is connected to the hall, then we would like the reverse to be true as well.

For now, we will just add one-way doors to the program; we will address the symmetry problem again in the next chapter and resolve it in chapter 5.

```
door(office, hall).
door(kitchen, office).
door(hall, 'dining room').
door(kitchen, cellar).
door('dining room', kitchen).
```

Here are some other facts about properties of things the game player might try to eat.

```
edible(apple).
edible(crackers).

tastes_yucky(broccoli).
```

Finally we define the initial status of the flashlight, and the player's location at the beginning of the game.

```
turned_off(flashlight).
here(kitchen).
```

We have now seen how to use basic facts to represent data in a Prolog program.

Exercises

During the course of completing the exercises you will develop
three Prolog applications in addition to Nani Search. The exercises
from each chapter will build on the work of previous chapters.
Suggested solutions to the exercises are contained in the Prolog
source files listed in the appendix, and are also included in the
Prolog samples directory, PROSAMP. The files are

family	A genealogical intelligent database
custord	A customer order entry application
birds	An expert system that identifies birds

Not all applications will be covered in each chapter. For example,
the expert system requires an understanding of rules and will not
be started until the end of chapter 5.

Genealogical Database

1- First create a source file for the genealogical database
application. Start by adding a few members of your family tree. It
is important to be accurate, since we will be exploring family
relationships. Your own knowledge of who your relatives are will
verify the correctness of your Prolog programs.

Start by recording the gender of the individuals. Use two separate
predicates, male/1 and female/1. For example, the FAMILY.PRO
file contains the facts

```
male(dennis).
male(michael).

female(diana).
```

Remember, if you want to include uppercase characters or
embedded blanks you must enclose the name in single (not double)
quotes. For example

```
male('Ghenghis Khan').
```

2- Enter a two-argument predicate that records the parent-child relationship. One argument represents the parent, and the other the child. It doesn't matter in which order you enter the arguments, as long as you are consistent. Often Prolog programmers adopt the convention that parent(A,B) is interpreted "A is the parent of B". For example

```
parent(dennis, michael).
parent(dennis, diana).
```

Customer Order Entry

3- Create a source file for the customer order entry program. We will begin it with three record types (predicates). The first is customer/3 where the three arguments are

arg1	Customer name
arg2	City
arg3	Credit rating (aaa, bbb, etc)

Add as many customers as you see fit.

4- Next add clauses that define the items that are for sale. It should also have three arguments

arg1	Item identification number
arg2	Item name
arg3	The reorder point for inventory (when at or below this level, reorder)

5- Next add an inventory record for each item. It has two arguments.

arg1	Item identification number (same as in the item record)
arg2	Amount in stock

3- Simple Queries

Now that we have some facts in our Prolog program, we can consult the program in the listener and query, or call, the facts. This chapter, and the next, will assume the Prolog program contains only facts. Queries against programs with rules will be covered in a later chapter.

Prolog queries work by pattern matching. The query pattern is called a goal. If there is a fact that matches the goal, then the query succeeds and the listener responds with 'yes.' If there is no matching fact, then the query fails and the listener responds with 'no.'

Prolog's pattern matching is called unification. In the case where the database contains only facts, unification succeeds if the following three conditions hold.

The predicate named in the goal and database are the same.

- Both predicates have the same arity.
- All of the arguments are the same.
- Before proceeding, review figure 3.1, which has a listing of the program so far.

The first query we will look at asks if the office is a room in the game. To pose this, we would enter that goal followed by a period at the listener prompt.

```
?- room(office).
yes
```

Prolog will respond with a 'yes' if a match was found. If we wanted to know if the attic was a room, we would enter that goal.

```
?- room(attic).
no
```

```
room(kitchen).
room(office).
room(hall).
```

```
room('dining room').
room(cellar).

door(office, hall).
door(kitchen, office).
door(hall, 'dining room').
door(kitchen, cellar).
door('dining room', kitchen).

location(desk, office).
location(apple, kitchen).
location(flashlight, desk).
location('washing machine', cellar).
location(nani, 'washing machine').
location(broccoli, kitchen).
location(crackers, kitchen).
location(computer, office).

edible(apple).
edible(crackers).

tastes_yucky(broccoli).

here(kitchen).
```

Figure 3.1. The listing of Nani Search entered at this point

Prolog will respond with a 'no' if no match was found. Likewise, we can ask about the locations of things.

```
?- location(apple, kitchen).
yes
```

```
?- location(kitchen, apple).
no
```

Prolog responds to our location query patterns in a manner that makes sense to us. That is, the kitchen is not located in the apple.

However, here is the problem with the one-way doors, which we still haven't fixed. It is mentioned again to stress the importance of the order of the arguments.

```
?- door(office, hall).
yes
```

```
?- door(hall, office).
no
```

Goals can be generalized by the use of Prolog variables. They do not behave like the variables in other languages, and are better called logical variables (although Prolog does not precisely correspond to logic). The logical variables replace one or more of the arguments in the goal.

Logical variables add a new dimension to unification. As before, the predicate names and arity must be the same for unification to succeed. However, when the corresponding arguments are compared, a variable will successfully match any term.

After successful unification, the logical variable takes on the value of the term it was matched with. This is called binding the variable. When a goal with a variable successfully unifies with a fact in the database, Prolog returns the value of the newly bound variable.

Since there may be more than one value a variable can be bound to and still satisfy the goal, Prolog provides the means for you to ask for alternate values. After an answer you can enter a semicolon (;). It causes Prolog to look for alternative bindings for the variables. Entering anything else at the prompt ends the query.

For example, we can use a logical variable to find all of the rooms.

```
?- room(X).
X = kitchen ;
X = office ;
X = hall ;
X = 'dining room' ;
X = cellar ;
no
```

The last 'no' means there are no more answers.

Here's how to find all the things in the kitchen. (Remember, variables begin with uppercase letters.)

```
?- location(Thing, kitchen).
Thing = apple ;
Thing = broccoli ;
Thing = crackers ;
no
```

We can use two variables to see everything in every place.

```
?- location(Thing, Place).
Thing = desk
Place = office ;

Thing = apple
Place = kitchen ;

Thing = flashlight
Place = desk ;

...
no
```

Other applications might have the following queries.

What customers live in Boston, and what is their credit rating?

```
?- customer(X, boston, Y).
```

What is the title of chapter 2?

```
?- chapter(2,Title).
```

What are the coordinates of window main?

```
?- window(main,Row1,Col1,Row2,Col2).
```

How Queries Work

When Prolog tries to satisfy a goal about a predicate, such as location/2, it searches through the clauses defining location/2. When it finds a match for its variables, it marks the particular clause that was used to satisfy the goal. Then, if the user asks for more answers, it resumes its search of the clauses at that place marker.

Referring to the list of clauses in figure 3.1, let's look closer at this process with the query location(X, kitchen). First, unification is attempted between the query pattern and the first clause of location/2.

Pattern   Clause #1

location(X, kitchen)   location(desk, office)

This unification fails. The predicate names are the same, the number of arguments is the same, but the second argument in the pattern, kitchen, is different from the second argument in the clause, office.

Next, unification is attempted between the pattern and the second clause of location/2.

Pattern   Clause #2

location(X, kitchen)   location(apple, kitchen)

This unification succeeds. The predicate names, arity (number of arguments), and second arguments are the same. The first arguments can be made the same if the variable X in the pattern takes the value 'apple.'

Now that unification succeeds, the Prolog listener reports its success, and the binding of the variable X.

```
?- location(X, kitchen).
X = apple
```

If the user presses a key other than the semicolon (;) at this point, the listener responds with 'yes' indicating the query ended successfully.

If the user presses the semicolon (;) key, the listener looks for other solutions. First it unbinds the variable X. Next it resumes the search using the clause following the one that had just satisfied the query. This is called backtracking. In the example that would be the third clause.

Pattern   Clause #3

location(X, kitchen)   location(flashlight, desk)

This fails, and the search continues. Eventually the sixth clause succeeds.

Pattern   Clause #6

location(X, kitchen)   location(broccoli, kitchen)

As a result, the variable X is now rebound to broccoli, and the listener responds

```
X = broccoli ;
```

Again, entering a semicolon (;) causes X to be unbound and the search to continue with the seventh clause, which also succeeds.

```
X = crackers ;
```

As before, entering anything except a semicolon (;) causes the listener to respond 'yes,' indicating success. A semicolon (;) causes the unbinding of X and the search to continue. But now, there are no more clauses that successfully unify with the pattern, so the listener responds with 'no' indicating the final attempt has failed.

```
no
```

The best way to understand Prolog execution is to trace its execution in the debugger. But first it is necessary to have a deeper understanding of goals.

A Prolog goal has four ports representing the flow of control through the goal: call, exit, redo, and fail. First the goal is called. If successful it is exited. If not it fails. If the goal is retried, by entering a semicolon (;) the redo port is entered. Figure 3.2 shows the goal and its ports.

Figure 3.2. The ports of a Prolog goal

The behaviors at each port are

call

Begins searching for clauses that unify with the goal

exit

Indicates the goal is satisfied, sets a place marker at the clause and binds the variables appropriately

redo

Retries the goal, unbinds the variables and resumes search at the place marker

fail

Indicates no more clauses match the goal

Prolog debuggers use these ports to describe the state of a query. Figure 3.3 shows a trace of the location(X, kitchen) query. Study it carefully because it is the key to your understanding of Prolog. The number in parentheses indicates the current clause.

```
?- location(X, kitchen).

CALL: - location(X, kitchen)
EXIT:(2) location(apple, kitchen)
  X = apple ;
REDO: location(X, kitchen)
EXIT:(6) location(broccoli, kitchen)
  X = broccoli ;
REDO: location(X, kitchen)
EXIT:(7) location(crackers, kitchen)
  X = crackers ;
FAIL - location(X, kitchen)
  no
```

Figure 3.3. Prolog trace of location(X, kitchen)

Because the trace information presented in this book is designed to teach Prolog rather than debug it, the format is a little different from that used in the actual debugger. Run the Amzi! debugger on these queries to see how they work for real.

To start the Amzi! debugger, select Listener/Debug On from the main menu of the IDE, or enter the debug command at the listener prompt.

```
?- debug.
```

You will see a separate window appear that contains trace information. Enter the query 'location(X, kitchen)' in the listener window. You will see the trace start in the debugger window. (Turn 'format' off to get trace output that looks like the output in the book.)

Use the 'Creep' button in the debugger to creep from port to port. When output appears in the listener window, enter semicolons (;) to continue the search. See the help files for more details on the debugger.

Unification between goals and facts is actually more general than has been presented. Variables can also occur in the facts of the Prolog database as well.

For example, the following fact could be added to the Prolog program. It might mean everyone sleeps.

```
sleeps(X).
```

You can add it directly in the listener, to experiment with, like this.

?- assert(sleeps(X)).

yes

Queries against a database with this fact give the following results.

```
?- sleeps(jane).
yes
```

```
?- sleeps(tom).
yes
```

Notice that the listener does not return the variable bindings of 'X=jane' and 'X=tom.' While they are surely bound that way, the listener only lists variables mentioned in the query, not those used in the program.

Prolog can also bind variables to variables.

```
?- sleeps(Z).
Z = H116

?- sleeps(X).
X = H247
```

When two unbound variables match, they are both bound, but not to a value! They are bound together, so that if either one takes a value, the other takes the same value. This is usually implemented by binding both variables to a common internal variable. In the first query above, both Z in the query and X in the fact are bound to internal variable 'H116.' In this way Prolog remembers they have the same value. If either one is bound to a value later on, both automatically bind to that value. This feature of Prolog distinguishes it from other languages and, as we will discover later, gives Prolog much of its power.

The two queries above are the same, even though one uses the same character X that is used in the fact sleeps(X). The variable in the fact is considered different from the one in the query.

Exercises

The exercise sections will often contain nonsense Prolog questions. These are queries against a meaningless database to strengthen your understanding of Prolog without the benefit of meaningful semantics. You are to predict the answers to the query and then try them in Prolog to see if you are correct. If you are not, trace the queries to better understand them.

Nonsense Prolog

1- Consider the following Prolog database

```
easy(1).
easy(2).
easy(3).

gizmo(a,1).
gizmo(b,3).
gizmo(a,2).
gizmo(d,5).
gizmo(c,3).
gizmo(a,3).
gizmo(c,4).
```

and predict the answers to the queries below, including all alternatives when the semicolon (;) is entered after an answer.

```
?- easy(2).
?- easy(X).

?- gizmo(a,X).
?- gizmo(X,3).
?- gizmo(d,Y).
?- gizmo(X,X).
```

2- Consider this database,

```
harder(a,1).
harder(c,X).
harder(b,4).
harder(d,2).
```

and predict the answers to these queries.

```
?- harder(a,X).
?- harder(c,X).
?- harder(X,1).
```

```
?- harder(X,4).
```

Adventure Game

3- Enter the listener and reproduce some of the example queries you have seen against location/2. List or print location/2 for reference if you need it. Remember to respond with a semicolon (;) for multiple answers. Trace the query.

Genealogical Database

4- Pose queries against the genealogical database that:

- Confirm a parent relationship such as parent(dennis, diana)
- Find someone's parent such as parent(X, diana)
- Find someone's children such as parent(dennis, X)
- List all parent-children such as parent(X,Y)

5- If parent/2 seems to be working, you can add additional family members to get a larger database. Remember to include the corresponding male/1 or female/1 predicate for each individual added.

Customer Order Entry

6- Pose queries against the customer order entry database that

- find customers in a given city
- find customers with a given credit rating
- confirm a given customer's credit rating
- find the customers in a given city with a given credit rating
- find the reorder quantity for a given item
- find the item number for a given item name
- find the inventory level for a given item number

4- Compound Queries

Simple goals can be combined to form compound queries. For example, we might want to know if there is anything good to eat in the kitchen. In Prolog we might ask

```
?- location(X, kitchen), edible(X).
```

Whereas a simple query had a single goal, the compound query has a conjunction of goals. The comma separating the goals is read as "and."

Logically (declaratively) the example means "Is there an X such that X is located in the kitchen and X is edible?" If the same variable name appears more than once in a query, it must have the same value in all places it appears. The query in the above example will only succeed if there is a single value of X that can satisfy both goals.

However, the variable name has no significance to any other query, or clause in the database. If X appears in other queries or clauses, that query or clause gets its own copy of the variable. We say the scope of a logical variable is a query.

Trying the sample query we get

```
?- location(X, kitchen), edible(X).
X = apple ;
X = crackers ;
no
```

The 'broccoli' does not show up as an answer because we did not include it in the edible/1 predicate.

This logical query can also be interpreted procedurally, using an understanding of Prolog's execution strategy. The procedural interpretation is: "First find an X located in the kitchen, and then test to see if it is edible. If it is not, go back and find another X in the kitchen and test it. Repeat until successful, or until there are no more Xs in the kitchen."

To understand the execution of a compound query, think of the goals as being arranged from left to right. Also think of a separate table which is kept for the current variable bindings. The flow of control moves back and forth through the goals as Prolog attempts to find variable bindings that satisfy the query.

Each goal can be entered from either the left or the right, and can be left from either the left or the right. These are the ports of the goal as seen in the last chapter.

A compound query begins by calling the first goal on the left. If it succeeds, the next goal is called with the variable bindings as set from the previous goal. If the query finishes via the exit port of the rightmost goal, it succeeds, and the listener prints the values in the variable table.

If the user types semicolon (;) after an answer, the query is re-entered at the redo port of the rightmost goal. Only the variable bindings that were set in that goal are undone.

If the query finishes via the fail port of the leftmost goal, the query fails. Figure 4.1 shows a compound query with the listener interaction on the ending ports.

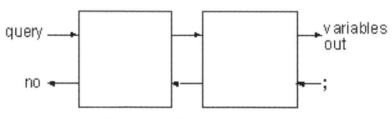

Figure 4.1. Compound queries

Figure 4.2 contains the annotated trace of the sample query. Make sure you understand it before proceeding.

```
?- location(X, kitchen), edible(X).
```

The trace has a new feature, which is a number in the first column that indicates the goal being worked on.

First the goal location(X, kitchen) is called, and the trace indicates that pattern matches the second clause of location.

```
1 CALL location(X, kitchen)
```

It succeeds, and results in the binding of X to apple.

```
1 EXIT (2)location(apple, kitchen)
```

Next, the second goal edible(X) is called. However, X is now bound to apple, so it is called as edible(apple).

```
2 CALL edible(apple)
```

It succeeds on the first clause of edible/1, thus exiting the query successfully.

```
2 EXIT (1) edible(apple)
   X = apple ;
```

Entering semicolon (;) causes the listener to backtrack into the rightmost goal of the query.

```
2 REDO edible(apple)
```

There are no other clauses that match this pattern, so it fails.

```
2 FAIL edible(apple)
```

Leaving the fail port of the second goal causes the listener to enter the redo port of the first goal. In so doing, the variable binding that was established by that goal is undone, leaving X unbound.

```
1 REDO location(X, kitchen)
```

It now succeeds at the sixth clause, rebinding X to broccoli.

1 EXIT (6) location(broccoli, kitchen)

The second goal is called again with the new variable binding. This is a fresh call, just as the first one was, and causes the search for a match to begin at the first clause.

2 CALL edible(broccoli)

There is no clause for edible(broccoli), so it fails.

2 FAIL edible(broccoli)

The first goal is then re-entered at the redo port, undoing the variable binding.

1 REDO location(X, kitchen)

It succeeds with a new variable binding.

1 EXIT (7) location(crackers, kitchen)

This leads to the second solution to the query.

2 CALL edible(crackers)
2 EXIT (2) edible(crackers)
   X = crackers ;

Typing semicolon (;) initiates backtracking again, which fails through both goals and leads to the ultimate failure of the query.

2 REDO edible(crackers)
2 FAIL edible(crackers)
1 REDO location(X, kitchen)
1 FAIL location(X, kitchen)
   no

Figure 4.2. Annotated trace of compound query

In this example we had a single variable, which was bound (given a value) by the first goal and tested in the second goal. We will now look at a more general example with two variables. It is attempting to ask for all the things located in rooms adjacent to the kitchen.

In logical terms, the query says "Find a T and R such that there is a door from the kitchen to R and T is located in R." In procedural terms it says "First find an R with a door from the kitchen to R. Use that value of R to look for a T located in R."

```
?- door(kitchen, R), location(T,R).
R = office
T = desk ;

R = office
T = computer ;

R = cellar
T = 'washing machine' ;
no
```

In this query, the backtracking is more complex. Figure 4.3 shows its trace.

Notice that the variable R is bound by the first goal and T is bound by the second. Likewise, the two variables are unbound by entering the redo port of the goal that bound them. After R is first bound to office, that binding sticks during backtracking through the second goal. Only when the listener backtracks into the first goal does R get unbound.

```
Goal: door(kitchen, R), location(T,R)

1 CALL door(kitchen, R)
1 EXIT (2) door(kitchen, office)
2 CALL location(T, office)
2 EXIT (1) location(desk, office)
    R = office
    T = desk ;
2 REDO location(T, office)
2 EXIT (8) location(computer, office)
    R = office
    T = computer ;
2 REDO location(T, office)
```

```
2 FAIL location(T, office)
1 REDO door(kitchen, R)
1 EXIT (4) door(kitchen, cellar)
2 CALL location(T, cellar)
2 EXIT (4) location('washing machine', cellar)
   R = cellar
   T = 'washing machine' ;
2 REDO location(T, cellar)
2 FAIL location(T, cellar)
1 REDO door(kitchen, R)
1 FAIL door(kitchen, R)
   no
```

Figure 4.3. Trace of a compound query

Built-in Predicates

Up to this point we have been satisfied with the format Prolog uses to give us answers. We will now see how to generate output that is customized to our needs. The example will be a query that lists all of the items in the kitchen. This will require performing I/O and forcing the listener to automatically backtrack to find all solutions.

To do this, we need to understand the concept of the built-in (evaluable) predicate. A built-in predicate is predefined by Prolog. There are no clauses in the database for built-in predicates. When the listener encounters a goal that matches a built-in predicate, it calls a predefined procedure.

Built-in predicates are usually written in the language used to implement the listener. They can perform functions that have nothing to do with logical theorem proving, such as writing to the console. For this reason they are sometimes called extra-logical predicates.

However, since they appear as Prolog goals they must be able to respond to either a call from the left or a redo from the right. Its response in the redo case is referred to as its behavior on backtracking.

We will introduce specific built-in predicates as we need them.

Here are the I/O predicates that will let us control the output of our query.

write/1   This predicate always succeeds when called, and has the side effect of writing its argument to the console. It always fails on backtracking. Backtracking does not undo the side effect.

nl/0   Succeeds, and starts a new line. Like write, it always succeeds when called, and fails on backtracking.

tab/1   It expects the argument to be an integer and tabs that number of spaces. It succeeds when called and fails on backtracking.

Figure 4.4 is a stylized picture of a goal showing its internal control structure. We will compare this with the internal flow of control of various built-in predicates.

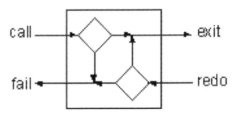

Figure 4.4. Internal flow of control through a normal goal

In figure 4.4, the upper left diamond represents the decision point after a call. Starting with the first clause of a predicate, unification is attempted between the query pattern and each clause, until either unification succeeds or there are no more clauses to try. If unification succeeded, branch to exit, marking the clause that successfully unified, if it failed, branch to fail.

The lower right diamond represents the decision point after a redo. Starting with the most recent clause found in the predicate, unification is again attempted between the query pattern and remaining clauses. If it succeeds, branch to exit, if not, branch to fail.

The I/O built-in predicates differ from normal goals in that they never change the direction of the flow of control. If they get control from the left, they pass control to the right. If they get control from the right, they pass control to the left as shown in figure 4.5.

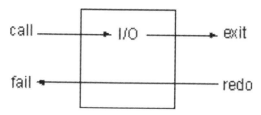

Figure 4.5. Internal flow of control through an I/O predicate

The output I/O predicates do not affect the variable table; however, they may output values from it. They simply leave their mark at the console each time control passes through them from left to right.

There are built-in predicates that do affect backtracking, and we have need of one of them for the first example. It is fail/0, and, as its name implies, it always fails.

If fail/0 gets control from the left, it immediately passes control back to the redo port of the goal on the left. It will never get control from the right, since it never allows control to pass to its right. Figure 4.6 shows its internal control structure.

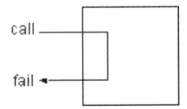

Figure 4.6. Internal flow of control through the fail/0 predicate

Previously we relied on the listener to display variable bindings for us, and used the semicolon (;) response to generate all of the possible solutions. We can now use the I/O built-in predicates to display the variable bindings, and the fail/0 predicate to force backtracking so all solutions are displayed.

Here then is the query that lists everything in the kitchen.

```
?- location(X, kitchen), write(X) ,nl,
fail.
   apple
   broccoli
   crackers
   no
```

The final 'no' means the query failed, as it was destined to, due to the fail/0.

Figure 4.7 shows the control flow through this query.

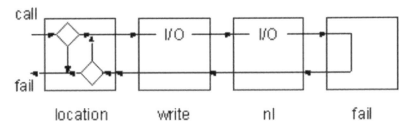

Figure 4.7. Flow of control through query with built-in predicates

Figure 4.8 shows a trace of the query.

```
Goal: location(X, kitchen), write(X), nl, fail.

1 CALL location(X, kitchen)
1 EXIT (2) location(apple, kitchen)
2 CALL write(apple)
    apple
2 EXIT write(apple)
3 CALL nl

3 EXIT nl
4 CALL fail
4 FAIL fail
3 REDO nl
3 FAIL nl
2 REDO write(apple)
2 FAIL write(apple)
1 REDO location(X, kitchen)
1 EXIT (6) location(broccoli, kitchen)
2 CALL write(broccoli)
    broccoli
2 EXIT write(broccoli)
3 CALL nl

3 EXIT nl
4 CALL fail
4 FAIL fail
3 REDO nl
3 FAIL nl
2 REDO write(broccoli)
2 FAIL write(broccoli)
1 REDO location(X, kitchen)
1 EXIT (7) location(crackers, kitchen)
2 CALL write(crackers)
    crackers
2 EXIT write(crackers)
3 CALL nl

3 EXIT nl
4 CALL fail
4 FAIL fail
3 REDO nl
3 FAIL nl
2 REDO write(crackers)
```

```
2 FAIL write(crackers)
1 REDO location(X, kitchen)
1 FAIL location(X, kitchen)
   no
```
Figure 4.8. Trace of query with built-in predicates

Exercises
Nonsense Prolog

1- Consider the following Prolog database.

```
easy(1).
easy(2).
easy(3).

gizmo(a,1).
gizmo(b,3).
gizmo(a,2).
gizmo(d,5).
gizmo(c,3).
gizmo(a,3).
gizmo(c,4).

harder(a,1).
harder(c,X).
harder(b,4).
harder(d,2).
```

Predict the results of the following queries. Then try them and trace them to see if you were correct.

```
?- gizmo(a,X),easy(X).
?- gizmo(c,X),easy(X).
?- gizmo(d,Z),easy(Z).

?- easy(Y),gizmo(X,Y).

?- write('report'), nl, easy(T), write(T),
gizmo(M,T), tab(2), write(M), fail.
```

```
?- write('buggy'), nl, easy(Z), write(X),
gizmo(Z,X), tab(2), write(Z), fail.

?- easy(X),harder(Y,X).
?- harder(Y,X),easy(X).
```

Adventure Game

2- Experiment with the queries you have seen in this chapter.

3- Predict the results of this query before you execute it. Then try it. Trace it if you were wrong.

```
?- door(kitchen, R), write(R), nl,
location(T,R), tab(3), write(T), nl, fail.
```

Genealogical Database

4- Compound queries can be used to find family relationships in the genealogical database. For example, find someone's mother with

```
?- parent(X, someone), female(X).
```

Write similar queries for fathers, sons, and daughters. Trace these queries to understand their behavior (or misbehavior if they are not working right for you).

5- Experiment with the ordering of the goals. In particular, contrast the queries.

```
?- parent(X, someone), female(X).
?- female(X), parent(X, someone).
```

Do they both give the same answer? Trace both queries and see which takes more steps.

6- The same predicate can be used multiple times in the same query. For example, we can find grandparents

```
?- parent(X, someone), parent(GP, X).
```

7- Write queries which find grandmothers, grandfathers, and great-

great grandparents.

Customer Order Entry

8- Write a query against the item and inventory records that returns
the inventory level for an item when you only know the item name.

5- Rules

We said earlier a predicate is defined by clauses, which may be facts or rules. A rule is no more than a stored query. Its syntax is

```
head :- body.
```

where

head	a predicate definition (just like a fact)
:-	the neck symbol, sometimes read as "if"
body	one or more goals (a query)

For example, the compound query that finds out where the good things to eat are can be stored as a rule with the predicate name where_food/2.

```
where_food(X,Y) :-
    location(X,Y),
    edible(X).
```

It states "There is something X to eat in room Y if X is located in Y, and X is edible."

We can now use the new rule directly in a query to find things to eat in a room. As before, the semicolon (;) after an answer is used to find all the answers.

```
?- where_food(X, kitchen).
X = apple ;
X = crackers ;
no

?- where_food(Thing, 'dining room').
no
```

Or it can check on specific things.

```
?- where_food(apple, kitchen).
yes
```

Or it can tell us everything.

```
?- where_food(Thing, Room).
Thing = apple
Room = kitchen ;

Thing = crackers
Room = kitchen ;
no
```

Just as we had multiple facts defining a predicate, we can have multiple rules for a predicate. For example, we might want to have the broccoli included in where_food/2. (Prolog doesn't have an opinion on whether or not broccoli is legitimate food. It just matches patterns.) To do this we add another where_food/2 clause for things that 'taste_yucky.'

```
where_food(X,Y) :-
   location(X,Y),
   edible(X).
where_food(X,Y) :-
   location(X,Y),
   tastes_yucky(X).
```

Now the broccoli shows up when we use the semicolon (;) to ask for everything.

```
?- where_food(X, kitchen).
X = apple ;
X = crackers ;
X = broccoli ;
no
```

Until this point, when we have seen Prolog try to satisfy goals by searching the clauses of a predicate, all of the clauses have been facts.

How Rules Work

With rules, Prolog unifies the goal pattern with the head of the clause. If unification succeeds, then Prolog initiates a new query using the goals in the body of the clause.

Rules, in effect, give us multiple levels of queries. The first level is composed of the original goals. The next level is a new query composed of goals found in the body of a clause from the first level.

Each level can create even deeper levels. Theoretically, this could continue forever. In practice it can continue until the listener runs out of space.

Figure 5.1 shows the control flow after the head of a rule has been matched. Notice how backtracking from the third goal of the first level now goes into the second level.

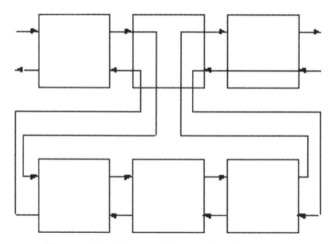

Figure 5.1. Control flow with rules

In this example, the middle goal on the first level succeeds or fails if its body succeeds or fails. When entered from the right (redo) the goal reenters its body query from the right (redo). When the query fails, the next clause of the first-level goal is tried, and if the next clause is also a rule, the process is repeated with the second clause's body.

As always with Prolog, these relationships become clearer by studying a trace. Figure 5.2 contains the annotated trace of the where_food/2 query. Notice the appearance of a two-part number. The first part of the number indicates the query level. The second part indicates the number of the goal within the query, as before. The parenthetical number is the clause number. For example

```
2-1 EXIT (7) location(crackers, kitchen)
```

means the exit occurred at the second level, first goal using clause number seven.

The query is

```
?- where_food(X, kitchen).
```

First the clauses of where_food/2 are searched.

```
1-1 CALL where_food(X, kitchen)
```

The pattern matches the head of the first clause, and while it is not at a port, the trace could inform us of the clause it is working on.

```
1-1 try (1) where_food(X, kitchen)
```

The body of the first clause is then set up as a query, and the trace continues.

```
   2-1 CALL location(X, kitchen)
```

From this point the trace proceeds exactly as it did for the compound query in the previous chapter.

```
   2-1 EXIT (2) location(apple, kitchen)
   2-2 CALL edible(apple)
   2-2 EXIT (1) edible(apple)
```

Since the body has succeeded, the goal from the previous (first) level succeeds.

```
1-1 EXIT (1) where_food(apple, kitchen)
      X = apple ;
```

Backtracking goes from the first-level goal, into the second level, proceeding as before.

```
1-1 REDO where_food(X, kitchen)
  2-2 REDO edible(apple)
  2-2 FAIL edible(apple)
  2-1 REDO location(X, kitchen)
  2-1 EXIT (6) location(broccoli, kitchen)
  2-2 CALL edible(broccoli)
  2-2 FAIL edible(broccoli)
  2-1 REDO location(X, kitchen)
  2-1 EXIT (7) location(crackers, kitchen)
  2-2 CALL edible(crackers)
  2-2 EXIT (2) edible(crackers)
1-1 EXIT (1) where_food(crackers, kitchen)
      X = crackers ;
```

Now any attempt to backtrack into the query will result in no more answers, and the query will fail.

```
  2-2 REDO edible(crackers)
  2-2 FAIL edible(crackers)
  2-1 REDO location(X, kitchen)
  2-1 FAIL location(X, kitchen)
```

This causes the listener to look for other clauses whose heads match the query pattern. In our example, the second clause of where_food/2 also matches the query pattern.

```
1-1 REDO where_food(X, kitchen)
```

Again, although traces usually don't tell us so, it is building a query from the body of the second clause.

```
1-1 try (2) where_food(X, kitchen)
```

Now the second query proceeds as normal, finding the broccoli, which tastes_yucky.

```
  2-1 CALL location(X, kitchen)
  2-1 EXIT (2) location(apple, kitchen)
  2-2 CALL tastes_yucky(apple)
  2-2 FAIL tastes_yucky(apple)
  2-1 REDO location(X, kitchen)
  2-1 EXIT (6) location(broccoli, kitchen)
  2-2 CALL tastes_yucky(broccoli)
```

```
  2-2 EXIT (1) tastes_yucky(broccoli)
1-1 EXIT (2) where_food(broccoli, kitchen)
     X = broccoli ;
```

Backtracking brings us to the ultimate no, as there
are no more where_food/2 clauses to try.

```
  2-2 REDO tastes_yucky(broccoli)
  2-2 FAIL tastes_yucky(broccoli)
  2-1 REDO location(X,kitchen)
  2-1 EXIT (7) location(crackers, kitchen)
  2-2 CALL tastes_yucky(crackers)
  2-2 FAIL tastes_yucky(crackers)
  2-2 REDO location(X, kitchen)
  2-2 FAIL location(X, kitchen)
1-1 REDO where_food(X, kitchen)
1-1 FAIL where_food(X, kitchen)
     no
```
Figure 5.2. Trace of a query with rules

It is important to understand the relationship between the first-level and second-level variables in this query. These are independent variables, that is, the X in the query is not the same as the X that shows up in the body of the where_food/2 clauses, values for both happen to be equal due to unification.

To better understand the relationship, we will slowly step through the process of transferring control. Subscripts identify the variable levels.

The goal in the query is

```
?- where_food(X1, kitchen)
```

The head of the first clause is

```
where_food(X2, Y2)
```

Remember the 'sleeps' example in chapter 3 where a query with a variable was unified with a fact with a variable? Both variables were set to be equal to each other. This is exactly what happens here. This might be implemented by setting both variables to a common internal variable. If either one takes on a new value, both take on a new value.

So, after unification between the goal and the head, the variable bindings are

```
X1 = _01
X2 = _01
Y2 = kitchen
```

The second-level query is built from the body of the clause, using these bindings.

```
location(_01, kitchen), edible(_01).
```

When internal variable _01 takes on a value, such as 'apple,' both X's then take on the same value. This is fundamentally different from the assignment statements that set variable values in most computer languages.

Using Rules

Using rules, we can solve the problem of the one-way doors. We can define a new two-way predicate with two clauses, called connect/2.

```
connect(X,Y) :- door(X,Y).
connect(X,Y) :- door(Y,X).
```

It says "Room X is connected to a room Y if there is a door from X to Y, or if there is a door from Y to X." Note the implied 'or' between clauses. Now connect/2 behaves the way we would like.

```
?- connect(kitchen, office).
yes

?- connect(office, kitchen).
yes
```

We can list all the connections (which is twice the number of doors) with a general query.

```
?- connect(X,Y).
```

```
X = office
Y = hall ;

X = kitchen
Y = office ;
...
X = hall
Y = office ;

X = office
Y = kitchen ;
...
```

With our current understanding of rules and built-in predicates we can now add more rules to Nani Search. We will start with look/0, which will tell the game player where he or she is, what things are in the room, and which rooms are adjacent.

To begin with, we will write list_things/1, which lists the things in a room. It uses the technique developed at the end of chapter 4 to loop through all the pertinent facts.

```
list_things(Place) :-
   location(X, Place),
   tab(2),
   write(X),
   nl,
   fail.
We use it like this.
?- list_things(kitchen).
   apple
   broccoli
   crackers
no
```

There is one small problem with list_things/1. It gives us the list, but it always fails. This is all right if we call it by itself, but we won't be able to use it in conjunction with other rules that follow it (to the right as illustrated in our diagrams). We can fix this problem by adding a second list_things/1 clause which always succeeds.

```
list_things(Place) :-
  location(X, Place),
  tab(2),
  write(X),
  nl,
  fail.
list_things(AnyPlace).
```

Now when the first clause fails (because there are no more location/2s to try) the second list_things/1 clause will be tried. Since its argument is a variable it will successfully match with anything, causing list_things/1 to always succeed and leave through the 'exit' port.

As with the second clause of list_things/1, it is often the case that we do not care what the value of a variable is, it is simply a place marker. For these situations there is a special variable called the anonymous variable, represented as an underscore (_). For example

```
list_things(_).
```

Next we will write list_connections/1, which lists connecting rooms. Since rules can refer to other rules, as well as to facts, we can write list_connections/1 just like list_things/1 by using the connection/2 rule.

```
list_connections(Place) :-
  connect(Place, X),
  tab(2),
  write(X),
  nl,
  fail.
list_connections(_).
```

Trying it gives us

```
?- list_connections(hall).
  dining room
  office
```

```
yes
```

Now we are ready to write look/0. The single fact here(kitchen)
tells us where we are in the game. (In chapter 7 we will see how to
move about the game by dynamically changing here/1.) We can
use it with the two list predicates to write the full look/0.

```
look :-
  here(Place),
  write('You are in the '), write(Place),
nl,
  write('You can see:'), nl,
  list_things(Place),
  write('You can go to:'), nl,
  list_connections(Place).
```

Given we are in the kitchen, this is how it works.

```
?- look.
You are in the kitchen
You can see:
  apple
  broccoli
  crackers
You can go to:
  office
  cellar
  dining room
yes
```

We now have an understanding of the fundamentals of Prolog, and
it is worth summarizing what we have learned so far. We have
seen the following about rules in Prolog.

- A Prolog program is a database of interrelated facts
and rules.
- The rules communicate with each other through
unification, Prolog's built-in pattern matcher.
- The rules communicate with the user through built-
in predicates such as write/1.
- The rules can be queried (called) individually from

the listener.

We have seen the following about Prolog's control flow.

- The execution behavior of the rules is controlled by Prolog's built-in backtracking search mechanism.
- We can force backtracking with the built-in predicate fail.
- We can force success of a predicate by adding a final clause with dummy variables as arguments and no body.

We now understand the following aspects of Prolog programming.

- Facts in the database (locations, doors, etc.) replace conventional data definition.
- The backtracking search (list_things/1) replaces the coding of many looping constructs.
- Passing of control through pattern matching (connect/2) replaces conditional test and branch structures.
- The rules can be tested individually, encouraging modular program development.
- Rules that call rules encourage the programming practices of procedure abstraction and data abstraction. (For example, look/0 doesn't know how list_things/1 works, or how the location data is stored.)

With this level of understanding, we can make a lot of progress on the exercise applications. Take some time to work with the programs to consolidate your understanding before moving on to the following chapters.

Exercises
Nonsense Prolog

1- Consider the following Prolog database.

```
a(a1,1).
```

```
a(A,2).
a(a3,N).

b(1,b1).
b(2,B).
b(N,b3).

c(X,Y)  :-  a(X,N),  b(N,Y).

d(X,Y)  :-  a(X,N),  b(Y,N).
d(X,Y)  :-  a(N,X),  b(N,Y).
```

Predict the answers to the following queries, then check them with Prolog, tracing.

```
?- a(X,2).

?- b(X,kalamazoo).

?- c(X,b3).
?- c(X,Y).

?- d(X,Y).
```

Adventure Game

2- Experiment with the various rules that were developed during this chapter, tracing them all.

3- Write look_in/1 for Nani Search. It should list the things located in its argument. For example, look_in(desk) should list the contents of the desk.

Genealogical Database

4- Build rules for the various family relationships that were developed as queries in the last chapter. For example

```
mother(M,C):-
   parent(M,C),
   female(M).
```

5- Build a rule for siblings. You will probably find your rule lists an individual as his/her own sibling. Use trace to figure out why.

6- We can fix the problem of individuals being their own siblings by using the built-in predicate that succeeds if two values are unequal, and fails if they are the same. The predicate is \=(X,Y). Jumping ahead a bit (to operator definitions in chapter 12), we can also write it in the form X \= Y.

7- Use the sibling predicate to define additional rules for brothers, sisters, uncles, aunts, and cousins.

8- If we want to represent marriages in the family database, we run into the two-way door problem we encountered in Nani Search. Unlike parent/2, which has two arguments with distinct meanings, married/2 can have the arguments reversed without changing the meaning.

Using the Nani Search door/2 predicate as an example, add some basic family data with a spouse/2 predicate. Then write the predicate married/2 using connect/2 as a model.

9- Use the new married predicate to add rules for uncles and aunts that get uncles and aunts by marriage as well as by blood. You should have two rules for each of these relationships, one for the blood case and one for the marriage case. Use trace to follow their behavior.

10- Explore other relationships, such as those between in-laws.

11- Write a predicate for grandparent/2. Use it to find both a grandparent and a grandchild.

```
grandparent(someone, X).
grandparent(X, someone).
```

Trace its behavior for both uses. Depending on how you wrote it, one use will require many more steps than the other. Write two predicates, one called grandparent/2 and one called grandchild/2. Order the goals in each so that they are efficient for their intended uses.

Customer Order Entry

12- Write a rule item_quantity/2 that is used to find the inventory level of a named item. This shields the user of this predicate from having to deal with the item numbers.

13- Write a rule that produces an inventory report using the item_quantity/2 predicate. It should display the name of the item and the quantity on hand. It should also always succeed. It will be similar to list_things/2.

14- Write a rule which defines a good customer. You might want to identify different cases of a good customer.

Expert Systems

Expert systems are often called rule-based systems. The rules are "rules of thumb" used by experts to solve certain problems. The expert system includes an inference engine, which knows how to use the rules.

There are many kinds of inference engines and knowledge representation techniques that are used in expert systems. Prolog is an excellent language for building any kind of expert system. However, certain types of expert systems can be built directly using Prolog's native rules. These systems are called structured selection systems.

The code listing for 'birds' in the appendix contains a sample system that can be used to identify birds. You will be asked to build a similar system in the exercises. It can identify anything, from animals to cars to diseases.

15- Decide what kind of expert system you would like to build, and add a few initial identification rules. For example, a system to identify house pets might have these rules.

```
pet(dog):- size(medium), noise(woof).
pet(cat):- size(medium), noise(meow).
pet(mouse):- size(small), noise(squeak).
```

16- For now, we can use these rules by putting the known facts in the database. For example, if we add size(medium) and noise(meow) and then pose the query pet(X) we will find X=cat.

Many Prologs allow clauses to be entered directly at the listener prompt, which makes using this expert system a little easier. The presence of the neck symbol (:-) signals to the listener that the input is a clause to be added. So to add facts directly to the listener workspace, they must be made into rules, as follows.

```
?- size(medium) :- true.
recorded

?- noise(meow) :- true.
recorded
```

Jumping ahead, you can also use assert/1 like this

```
?- assert(size(medium)).
yes
?- assert(noise(meow)).
yes
```

These examples use the predicates in the general form attribute(value). In this simple example, the pet attribute is deduced. The size and noise attributes must be given.

17- Improve the expert system by having it ask for the attribute/ values it can't deduce. We do this by first adding the rules

```
size(X):- ask(size, X).
noise(X):- ask(noise, X).
```

For now, ask/2 will simply check with the user to see if an attribute/value pair is true or false. It will use the built-in predicate read/1 which reads a Prolog term (ending in a period of course).

```
ask(Attr, Val):-
   write(Attr),tab(1),write(Val),
   tab(1),write('(yes/no)'),write(?),
   read(X),
   X = yes.
```

The last goal, X = yes, attempts to unify X and yes. If yes was read, then it succeeds, otherwise, it fails.

6- Arithmetic

Prolog must be able to handle arithmetic in order to be a useful general purpose programming language. However, arithmetic does not fit nicely into the logical scheme of things.

That is, the concept of evaluating an arithmetic expression is in contrast to the straight pattern matching we have seen so far. For this reason, Prolog provides the built-in predicate 'is' that evaluates arithmetic expressions. Its syntax calls for the use of operators, which will be described in more detail in chapter 12.

```
X is <arithmetic expression>
```

The variable X is set to the value of the arithmetic expression. On backtracking it is unassigned.

The arithmetic expression looks like an arithmetic expression in any other programming language.

Here is how to use Prolog as a calculator.

```
?- X is 2 + 2.
X = 4

?- X is 3 * 4 + 2.
X = 14
```

Parentheses clarify precedence.

```
?- X is 3 * (4 + 2).
X = 18

?- X is (8 / 4) / 2.
X = 1
```

In addition to 'is,' Prolog provides a number of operators that compare two numbers. These include 'greater than', 'less than', 'greater or equal than', and 'less or equal than.' They behave more logically, and succeed or fail according to whether the comparison is true or false. Notice the order of the symbols in the greater or equal than and less than or equal operators. They are specifically

constructed not to look like an arrow, so that you can use arrow
symbols in your programs without confusion.

```
X > Y
X < Y
X >= Y
X =< Y
```

Here are a few examples of their use.

```
?- 4 > 3.
yes

?- 4 < 3.
no

?- X is 2 + 2, X > 3.
X = 4

?- X is 2 + 2, 3 >= X.
no

?- 3+4 > 3*2.
yes
```

They can be used in rules as well. Here are two example
predicates. One converts centigrade temperatures to Fahrenheit,
the other checks if a temperature is below freezing.

```
c_to_f(C,F) :-
   F is C * 9 / 5 + 32.

freezing(F) :-
   F =< 32.
```

Here are some examples of their use.

```
?- c_to_f(100,X).
X = 212
yes

?- freezing(15).
```

```
yes

?- freezing(45).
no
```

Exercises
Customer Order Entry

1- Write a predicate valid_order/3 that checks whether a customer order is valid. The arguments should be customer, item, and quantity. The predicate should succeed only if the customer is a valid customer with a good credit rating, the item is in stock, and the quantity ordered is less than the quantity in stock.

2- Write a reorder/1 predicate which checks inventory levels in the inventory record against the reorder quantity in the item record. It should write a message indicating whether or not it's time to reorder.

7- Managing Data

We have seen that a Prolog program is a database of predicates, and so far we have entered clauses for those predicates directly in our programs. Prolog also allows us to manipulate the database directly and provides built-in predicates to perform this function. The main ones are

asserta(X)	Adds the clause X as the first clause for its predicate. Like the other I/O predicates, it always fails on backtracking and does not undo its work.
assertz(X)	Same as asserta/1, only it adds the clause X as the last clause for its predicate.
retract(X)	Removes the clause X from the database, again with a permanent effect that is not undone on backtracking.

The ability to manipulate the database is obviously an important feature for Nani Search. With it we can dynamically change the location of the player, as well as the stuff that has been picked up and moved.

We will first develop goto/1, which moves the player from one room to another. It will be developed from the top down, in contrast to look/0 which was developed from the bottom up.

When the player enters the command goto, we first check if they can go to the place and if so move them so they can look around the new place. Starting from this description of goto/1, we can write the main predicate.

```
goto(Place):-
   can_go(Place),
   move(Place),
   look.
```

Next we fill in the details. We can go to a room if it connects to where we are.

```
can_go(Place):-
  here(X),
  connect(X, Place).
```

We can test can_go/1 immediately (assuming we are in the kitchen).

```
?- can_go(office).
yes

?- can_go(hall).
no
```

Now, can_go/1 succeeds and fails as we want it to, but it would be nice if it gave us a message when it failed. By adding a second clause, which is tried if the first one fails, we can cause can_go/1 to write an error message. Since we want can_go/1 to fail in this situation we also need to add a fail to the second clause.

```
can_go(Place):-
    here(X),
    connect(X, Place).
can_go(Place):-
    write('You can''t get there from
here.'), nl,
    fail.
  This version of can_go/1 behaves as we
want.
  ?- can_go(hall).
You can't get there from here.
no
```

Next we develop move/1, which does the work of dynamically updating the database to reflect the new location of the player. It retracts the old clause for here/1 and replaces it with a new one. This way there will always be only one here/1 clause representing the current place. Because goto/1 calls can_go/1 before move/1, the new here/1 will always be a legal place in the game.

```
move(Place):-
```

```
    retract(here(X)),
    asserta(here(Place)).
```

We can now use goto/1 to explore the game environment. The output it generates is from look/0, which we developed in chapter 5.

```
?- goto(office).
You are in the office
You can see:
  desk
  computer
You can go to:
  hall
  kitchen
yes

?- goto(hall).
You are in the hall
You can see:
You can go to:
  dining room
  office
yes

?- goto(kitchen).
You can't get there from here.
no
```

We will also need 'asserta' and 'retract' to implement 'take' and 'put' commands in the game.

Here is take/1. For it we will define a new predicate, have/1, which has one clause for each thing the game player has. Initially, have/1 is not defined because the player is not carrying anything.

```
take(X):-
  can_take(X),
  take_object(X).
can_take/1 is analogous to can_go/1.
can_take(Thing) :-
```

```
    here(Place),
    location(Thing, Place).
  can_take(Thing) :-
    write('There is no '), write(Thing),
    write(' here.'),
    nl, fail.
```

take_object/1 is analogous to move/1. It retracts a location/2 clause and asserts a have/1 clause, reflecting the movement of the object from the place to the player.

```
  take_object(X):-
    retract(location(X,_)),
    asserta(have(X)),
    write('taken'), nl.
```

As we have seen, the variables in a clause are local to that clause. There are no global variables in Prolog, as there are in many other languages. The Prolog database serves that purpose. It allows all clauses to share information on a wider basis, replacing the need for global variables. 'asserts' and 'retracts' are the tools used to manipulate this global data.

As with any programming language, global data can be a powerful concept, easily overused. They should be used with care, since they hide the communication of information between clauses. The same code will behave differently if the global data is changed. This can lead to hard-to-find bugs.

Eliminating global data and the 'assert' and 'retract' capabilities of Prolog is a goal of many logic programmers. It is possible to write Prolog programs without modifying the database, thus eliminating the problem of global variables. This is done by carrying the information as arguments to the predicates. In the case of an adventure game, the complete state of the game could be represented as predicate arguments, with each command called with the current state and returning a new modified state. This approach will be discussed in more detail in chapter 14.

Although the database approach presented here may not be the purest method from a logical standpoint, it does allow for a very natural representation of this game application.

Various Prologs provide varying degrees of richness in the area of database manipulation. The built-in versions are usually unaffected by backtracking. That is, like the other I/O predicates, they perform their function when called and do nothing when entered from the redo port.

Sometimes it is desirable to have a predicate retract its assertions when the redo port is entered. It is easy to write versions of 'assert' and 'retract' that undo their work on backtracking.

```
backtracking_assert(X):-
    asserta(X).
backtracking_assert(X):-
    retract(X),fail.
```

The first time through, the first clause is executed. If a later goal fails, backtracking will cause the second clause to be tried. It will undo the work of the first and fail, thus giving the desired effect.

Exercises
Adventure Game

1- Write put/1 which retracts a have/1 clause and asserts a location/2 clause in the current room.

2- Write inventory/0 which lists the have/1 things.

3- Use goto/1, take/1, put/1, look/0, and inventory/0 to move about and examine the game environment so far.

4- Write the predicates turn_on/1 and turn_off/1 for Nani Search. They will be used to turn the flashlight on or off.

5- Add an open/closed status for each of the doors. Write open and close predicates that do the obvious. Fix can_go/1 to check whether a door is open and write the appropriate error message if its not.

Customer Order Entry

6- In the order entry application, write a predicate update_inventory/2 that takes an item name and quantity as input. Have it retract the old inventory amount, perform the necessary arithmetic and assert the new inventory amount.

NOTE: retract(inventory(item_id,Q)) binds Q to the old value, thus alleviating the need for a separate goal to get the old value of the inventory.

7- We can now use the various predicates developed for the customer order entry system to write a predicate that prompts the user for order information and generates the order. The predicate can be simply order/0.

order/0 should first prompt the user for the customer name, the item name and the quantity. For example

```
write('Enter customer name:'),read(C),
```

It should then use the rules for good_customer and valid_order to verify that this is a valid order. If so, it should assert a new type of record, order/3, which records the order information. It can then update_inventory and check whether its time to reorder.

The customer order entry application has been designed from the bottom up, since that is the way the material has been presented for learning. The order predicate should suggest that Prolog is an excellent tool for top-down development as well.

One could start with the concept that processing an order means reading the date, checking the order, updating inventory, and reordering if necessary. The necessary details of implementing these predicates could be left for later.

Expert System

8- The expert system currently asks for the same information over and over again. We can use the database to remember the answers to questions so that ask/2 doesn't re-ask something.

When ask/2 gets a yes or no answer to a question about an attribute-value pair, assert a fact in the form

```
known(Attribute, Value, YesNo).
```

Add a first clause to ask/2 that checks whether the answer is already known and, if so, succeeds. Add a second clause that checks if the answer is known to be false and, if so, fails.

The third clause makes sure the answer is not already known, and then asks the user as before. To do this, the built-in predicate not/1 is used. It fails if its argument succeeds.

```
not (known(Attr, Val, Answer))
```

8- Recursion

Recursion in any language is the ability for a unit of code to call itself, repeatedly, if necessary. Recursion is often a very powerful and convenient way of representing certain programming constructs.

In Prolog, recursion occurs when a predicate contains a goal that refers to itself.

As we have seen in earlier chapters, every time a rule is called, Prolog uses the body of the rule to create a new query with new variables. Since the query is a new copy each time, it makes no difference whether a rule calls another rule or itself.

A recursive definition (in any language, not just Prolog) always has at least two parts, a boundary condition and a recursive case.

The boundary condition defines a simple case that we know to be true. The recursive case simplifies the problem by first removing a layer of complexity, and then calling itself. At each level, the boundary condition is checked. If it is reached the recursion ends. If not, the recursion continues.

We will illustrate recursion by writing a predicate that can detect things which are nested within other things.

Currently our location/2 predicate tells us the flashlight is in the desk and the desk is in the office, but it does not indicate that the flashlight is in the office.

```
?- location(flashlight, office).
no
```

Using recursion, we will write a new predicate, is_contained_in/2, which will dig through layers of nested things, so that it will answer 'yes' if asked if the flashlight is in the office.

To make the problem more interesting, we will first add some more nested items to the game. We will continue to use the location predicate to put things in the desk, which in turn can have other things inside them.

```
location(envelope, desk).
location(stamp, envelope).
location(key, envelope).
```

To list all of things in the office, we would first have to list those things that are directly in the office, like the desk. We would then list the things in the desk, and the things inside the things in the desk.

If we generalize a room into being just another thing, we can state a two-part rule which can be used to deduce whether something is contained in (nested in) something else.

- A thing, T1, is contained in another thing, T2, if T1 is directly located in T2. (This is the boundary condition.)
- A thing, T1, is contained in another thing, T2, if some intermediate thing, X, is located in T2 and T1 is contained in X. (This is where we simplify and recurse.)

We will now express this in Prolog. The first rule translates into Prolog in a straightforward manner.

```
is_contained_in(T1,T2) :-
    location(T1,T2).
```

The recursive rule is also straightforward. Notice that it refers to itself.

```
is_contained_in(T1,T2) :-
    location(X,T2),
    is_contained_in(T1,X).
```

Now we are ready to try it.

```
?- is_contained_in(X, office).
X = desk ;
X = computer ;
X = flashlight ;
X = envelope ;
X = stamp ;
```

```
X = key ;
no

?- is_contained_in(envelope, office).
yes

?- is_contained_in(apple, office).
no
```

How Recursion Works

As in all calls to rules, the variables in a rule are unique, or scoped, to the rule. In the recursive case, this means each call to the rule, at each level, has its own unique set of variables. So the values of X, T1, and T2 at the first level of recursion are different from those at the second level.

However, unification between a goal and the head of a clause forces a relationship between the variables of different levels. Using subscripts to distinguish the variables, and internal Prolog variables, we can trace the relationships for a couple of levels of recursion.

First, the query goal is

```
?- is_contained_in(XQ, office).
```

The clause with variables for the first level of recursion is

```
is_contained_in(T11, T21) :-
   location(X1, T21),
   is_contained_in(T11, X1).
```

When the query is unified with the head of the clause, the variables become bound. The bindings are

```
XQ  = _01
T11 = _01
T21 = office
X1  = _02
```

Note particularly that X0 in the query becomes bound to T11 in the clause, so when a value of _01 is found, both variables are found.

With these bindings, the clause can be rewritten as

```
is_contained_in(_01, office) :-
   location(_02, office),
   is_contained_in(_01, _02).
```

When the location/2 goal is satisfied, with _02 = desk, the recursive call becomes

```
is_contained_in(_01, desk)
```

That goal unifies with the head of a new copy of the clause, at the next level of the recursion. After that unification the variables are

XQ = _01	T11 = _01	T12 = _01
	T21 = office	T22 = desk
	X1 = desk	X2 = _03

When the recursion finds a solution, such as 'envelope,' all of the T1s and X0 immediately take on that value. Figure 8.1 contains a full annotated trace of the query.

```
The query is

?- is_contained_in(X, office).

Each level of the recursion will have its own unique
variables, but as in all calls to rules, the
variables at a called level will be bound in some
relationship to the variables at the calling level.
In the following trace, we will use Prolog internal
variables, so we can see which variables are bound
together and which are not.  The items directly in
the office are found easily, as the variable _0 is
bound to X in the query and T1 in the rule.
```

```
1-1 CALL is_contained_in(_0, office)
1-1 try (1) is_contained_in(_0, office)
   2-1 CALL location(_0, office)
   2-1 EXIT location(desk, office)
1-1 EXIT is_contained_in(desk, office)
   X = desk ;
   2-1 REDO location(_0, office)
   2-1 EXIT location(computer, office)
1-1 EXIT is_contained_in(computer, office)
   X = computer ;
   2-1 REDO location(_0,office)
   2-1 FAIL location(_0,office)
```

When there are no more location(X, office) clauses,
the first clause of is_contained_in/2 fails, and the
second clause is tried. Notice that the call to
location does not have its first argument bound to
the same variable. It was X in the rule, and it gets
a new internal value, _4. T1 stays bound to _0.

```
1-1 REDO is_contained_in(_0, office)
1-1 try (2) is_contained_in(_0, office)
   2-1 CALL location(_4, office)
   2-1 EXIT location(desk, office)
```

When it initiates a new call to is_contained_in/2, it
behaves exactly as if we had performed the query
is_contained_in(X, desk) at the listener prompt. It
is, in effect, a completely new copy of
is_contained_in/2. This call will find all of the
things in the desk, just as the first level found all
things in the office.

```
   2-2 CALL is_contained_in(_0, desk)
   2-2 try (1) is_contained_in(_0, desk)
      3-1 CALL location(_0, desk)
      3-1 EXIT location(flashlight, desk)
```

Having found the flashlight at the second-level
is_contained_in/2, the answer propagates back up to
the first level copy of is_contained_in/2.

```
   2-2 EXIT is_contained_in(flashlight, desk)
1-1 EXIT is_contained_in(flashlight, office)
   X = flashlight ;
```

*Similarly, it finds the envelope at the second level
of recursion.*

```
3-1 REDO location(_0, desk)
3-1 EXIT location(envelope, desk)
2-2 EXIT is_contained_in(envelope, desk)
1-1 EXIT is_contained_in(envelope, office)
  X = envelope ;
```

*Having exhausted the things located in the desk, it
next begins to look for things within things located
in the desk.*

```
3-1 REDO location(_0, desk)
3-1 FAIL location(_0, desk)
2-2 REDO is_contained_in(_0, desk)
2-2 try (2) is_contained_in(_0, desk)
3-1 CALL location(_7, desk)
3-1 EXIT location(flashlight, desk)
```

*First, is there something in the flashlight? Both
clauses of is_contained_in/2 fail because there is
nothing located in the flashlight.*

```
3-2 CALL is_contained_in(_0, flashlight)
  4-1 CALL location(_0, flashlight)
  4-1 FAIL location(_0, flashlight)
3-2 REDO is_contained_in(_0, flashlight)
3-2 try (2) is_contained_in(_0, flashlight)
  4-1 CALL location(_11, flashlight)
  4-1 FAIL location(_11, flashlight)
3-2 FAIL is_contained_in(_0, flashlight)
```

*Next, it tries to find things in the envelope and
comes up with the stamp.*

```
3-1 REDO location(_7, desk)
3-1 EXIT location(envelope, desk)
3-2 CALL is_contained_in(_0, envelope)
  4-1 CALL location(_0, envelope)
  4-1 EXIT location(stamp, envelope)
3-2 EXIT is_contained_in(stamp, envelope)
2-2 EXIT is_contained_in(stamp, desk)
1-1 EXIT is_contained_in(stamp, office)
```

```
    X = stamp ;
```

And then the key.

```
    4-1 REDO location(_0,envelope)
    4-1 EXIT location(key, envelope)
  3-2 EXIT is_contained_in(key, envelope)
 2-2 EXIT is_contained_in(key, desk)
1-1 EXIT is_contained_in(key, office)
    X = key ;
```

And then it fails its way back to the beginning.

```
    3-2 REDO is_contained_in(_0, envelope)
    3-2 try (2) is_contained_in(_0, envelope)
    4-1 CALL location(_11, envelope)
    4-1 EXIT location(stamp, envelope)
    4-2 CALL is_contained_in(_0, stamp)
      5-1 CALL location(_0, stamp)
      5-1 FAIL location(_0, stamp)
    4-2 REDO is_contained_in(_0, stamp)
    4-2 try(2) is_contained_in(_0, stamp)
      5-1 CALL location(_14, stamp)
      5-1 FAIL location(_14, stamp)
    4-1 REDO location(_11, envelope)
    4-1 EXIT location(key, envelope)
    4-2 CALL is_contained_in(_0, key)
    4-2 try (1) is_contained_in(_0, key)
      5-1 CALL location(_0, key)
      5-1 FAIL location(_0, key)
    4-2 REDO is_contained_in(_0, key)
    4-2 try (2) is_contained_in(_0, key)
      5-1 CALL location(_14, key)
      5-1 FAIL location(_14, key)
    4-1 REDO location(_7, desk)
    4-1 FAIL location(_7, desk)
  3-1 REDO location(_4, office)
  3-1 EXIT location(computer, office)
  3-2 CALL is_contained_in(_0, computer)
    4-1 CALL location(_0, computer)
    4-1 FAIL location(_0, computer)
  3-2 REDO is_contained_in(_0, computer)
    4-1 CALL location(_7, computer)
    4-1 FAIL location(_7, computer)
  3-1 REDO location(_4, office)
```

```
    3-1 FAIL location(_4, office)
  no
```
Figure 8.1. Trace of a recursive query

When writing a recursive predicate, it is essential to ensure that the boundary condition is checked at each level . Otherwise, the program might recurse forever.

The simplest way to do this is by always defining the boundary condition first, ensuring that it is always tried first and that the recursive case is only tried if the boundary condition fails.

Pragmatics

We now come to some of the pragmatics of Prolog programming. First consider that the goal location(X,Y) will be satisfied by every clause of location/2. On the other hand, the goals location(X, office) or location(envelope, X) will be satisfied by fewer clauses.

Let's look again at the second rule for is_contained_in/2, and an equally valid alternate coding.

```
is_contained_in(T1,T2):-
  location(X,T2),
  is_contained_in(T1,X).
```

```
is_contained_in(T1,T2):-
  location(T1,X),
  is_contained_in(X,T2).
```

Both will give correct answers, but the performance of each will depend on the query. The query is_contained_in(X, office) will execute faster with the first version. That is because T2 is bound, making the search for location(X, T2) easier than if both variables were unbound. Similarly, the second version is faster for queries such as is_contained_in(key, X).

Exercises
Adventure Game

1- Trace the two versions of is_contained_in/2 presented at the end of the chapter to understand the performance differences between them.

2- Currently, the can_take/1 predicate only allows the player to take things which are directly located in a room. Modify it so it uses the recursive is_contained_in/2 so that a player can take anything in a room.

Genealogical Database

3- Use recursion to write an ancestor/2 predicate. Then trace it to understand its behavior. It is possible to write endless loops with recursive predicates. The trace facility will help you debug ancestor/2 if it is not working correctly.

4- Use ancestor/2 for finding all of a person's ancestors and all of a person's descendants. Based on your experience with grandparent/2 and grandchild/2, write a descendant/2 predicate optimized for descendants, as opposed to ancestor/2, which is optimized for ancestors.

9- Data Structures

So far we have worked with facts, queries, and rules that use simple data structures. The arguments to our predicates have all been atoms or integers, the basic building blocks of Prolog. Examples of atoms we've used are

```
office, apple, flashlight, nani
```

These primitive data types can be combined to form arbitrarily complex data types called structures. A structure is composed of a functor and a fixed number of arguments. Its form is just like that of the goals and facts we've seen already (for good reason, we'll discover).

```
functor(arg1,arg2,...)
```

Each of the structure's arguments can be either a primitive data type or another structure. For example, the things in the game are currently represented using atoms, such as 'desk' or 'apple,' but we can use structures to create a richer representation of these things. The following structures describe the object and its color, size, and weight.

```
object(candle, red, small, 1).
object(apple, red, small, 1).
object(apple, green, small, 1).
object(table, blue, big, 50).
```

These structures could be used directly in the second argument of location/2, but for experimentation we will instead create a new predicate, location_s/2. Note that even though the structures describing the objects in the game are complex, they still take up only one argument in location_s/2.

```
location_s(object(candle, red, small, 1),
kitchen).
location_s(object(apple, red, small, 1),
kitchen).
location_s(object(apple, green, small, 1),
kitchen).
location_s(object(table, blue, big, 50),
```

kitchen).

Prolog variables are typeless, and can be bound as easily to structures as to atoms. In fact, an atom is just a simple structure with a functor and no arguments. So we can ask

```
?- location_s(X, kitchen).
X = object(candle, red, small, 1) ;
X = object(apple, red, small, 1) ;
X = object(apple, green, small, 1) ;
X = object(table, blue, big, 50) ;
no
```

We can also pick apart the structure with variables. We can now find all the red things in the kitchen.

```
?- location_s(object(X, red, S, W),
kitchen).
X = candle
S = small
W = 1 ;

X = apple
S = small
W = 1 ;
no
```

If we didn't care about the size and weight we could replace the size, S, and weight, W, variables with the anonymous variable (_).

```
?- location_s(object(X, red, _, _),
kitchen).
X = candle ;
X = apple ;
no
```

We can use these structures to add more realism to the game. For example, we can modify our can_take/1 predicate, developed in chapter 7, so that we can only take small objects.

```
can_take_s(Thing) :-
    here(Room),
    location_s(object(Thing, _, small,_),
```

Room).

We can also change the error messages to reflect the two reasons why a thing cannot be taken. To ensure that backtracking does not cause both errors to be displayed, we will construct each clause so its message is displayed only when its unique conditions are met. To do this, the built-in predicate not/1 is used. Its argument is a goal, and it succeeds if its argument fails, and fails if its argument succeeds. For example

```
?- not( room(office) ).
no

?- not( location(cabbage, 'living room') )
yes
```

Note that semantically, not in Prolog means the goal cannot be successfully solved with current database of facts and rules. Here is how we use not/1 in our new version, can_take_s/1.

```
can_take_s(Thing) :-
   here(Room),
   location_s(object(Thing, _, small, _),
Room).
  can_take_s(Thing) :-
   here(Room),
   location_s(object(Thing, _, big, _),
Room),
    write('The '), write(Thing),
    write(' is too big to carry.'), nl,
    fail.
  can_take_s(Thing) :-
   here(Room),
   not (location_s(object(Thing, _, _, _),
Room)),
    write('There is no '), write(Thing),
write(' here.'), nl,
    fail.
```

We can now try it, assuming we are in the kitchen.

```
?- can_take_s(candle).
```

```
yes

?- can_take_s(table).
The table is too big to carry.
no

?- can_take_s(desk).
There is no desk here.
no
```

The list_things/1 predicate can be modified to give a description of the things in a room.

```
list_things_s(Place) :-
   location_s(object(Thing, Color, Size,
Weight),Place),
    write('A '),write(Size),tab(1),
    write(Color),tab(1),
    write(Thing), write(', weighing '),
    write(Weight), write(' pounds'), nl,
    fail.
list_things_s(_).
```

Requesting it now gives a more detailed list.

```
?- list_things_s(kitchen).
A small red candle, weighing 1 pounds
A small red apple, weighing 1 pounds
A small green apple, weighing 1 pounds
A big blue table, weighing 50 pounds
yes
```

If you are bothered by the grammatically incorrect '1 pounds', you can fix it by adding another rule to write the weight, which would replace the direct 'writes' now used.

```
write_weight(1) :-
   write('1 pound').
write_weight(W) :-
   W > 1,
   write(W), write(' pounds').
```

Testing it shows it works as desired.

```
?- write_weight(4).
4 pounds
yes


?- write_weight(1).
1 pound
yes
```

Notice that we did not need to put a test, such as 'W = 1,' in the first clause. By putting the 1 directly in the argument at the head of the clause we ensure that that clause will only be fired when the query goal is write_weight(1). All other queries will go to the second clause because the goal pattern will fail to unify with the head of the first clause.

It is important, however, to put the test 'W > 1' in the second rule. Otherwise both rules would work for a weight of 1. The first time the predicate was called would not be a problem, but on backtracking we would get two answers if we had not included the test.

Structures can be arbitrarily complex, so if we wanted to get fancy about things in the game we could keep their dimensions (length, width, height) instead of their size as part of their description.

```
object(desk, brown, dimension(6,3,3), 90).
```

We can also use embedded structures for clarity.

```
object(desk, color(brown), size(large),
weight(90))
```

A query using these structures is more readable.

```
location_s(object(X, _, size(large), _),
office).
```

Notice that the position of the arguments is important. The place-holding anonymous variables are essential for getting the correct results.

Exercises
Adventure Game

1- Incorporate the new location into the game. Note that due to data and procedure abstraction, we need only change the low level predicates that deal directly with location. The higher level predicates, such as look/0 and take/1 are unaffected by the change.

Customer Order Entry

2- Use structures to enhance the customer order entry application. For example, include a structure for each customers address.

10- Unification

One of Prolog's most powerful features is its built-in pattern-matching algorithm, unification. For all of the examples we have seen so far, unification has been relatively simple. We will now examine unification more closely.

The full definition of unification is similar to the one given in chapter 3, with the addition of a recursive definition to handle data structures. This following table summarizes the unification process.

variable & any term	The variable will unify with and is bound to any term, including another variable.
primitive & primitive	Two primitive terms (atoms or integers) unify only if they are identical.
structure & structure	Two structures unify if they have the same functor and arity and if each pair of corresponding arguments unify.

In order to experiment with unification we will introduce the built-in predicate =/2, which succeeds if its two arguments unify and fails if they do not. It can be written in operator syntax as follows.

```
arg1 = arg2
```

which is equivalent to

```
=(arg1, arg2)
```

WARNING: The equal sign (=) does not cause assignment as in most programming languages, nor does it cause arithmetic evaluation. It causes Prolog unification. (Despite this warning, if you are like most mortal programmers, you will be tripped up by this difference more than once.)

Unification between two sides of an equal sign (=) is exactly the same as the unification that occurs when Prolog tries to match

goals with the heads of clauses. On backtracking, the variable
bindings are undone, just as they are when Prolog backtracks
through clauses.

The simplest form of unification occurs between two structures
with no variables. In this case, either they are identical and
unification succeeds, or they are not, and unification fails.

```
?- a = a.
yes

?- a = b.
no

?- location(apple, kitchen) =
location(apple, kitchen).
yes

?- location(apple, kitchen) =
location(pear, kitchen).
no

?- a(b,c(d,e(f,g))) = a(b,c(d,e(f,g))).
yes

?- a(b,c(d,e(f,g))) = a(b,c(d,e(g,f))).
no
```

Another simple form of unification occurs between a variable and a
primitive. The variable takes on a value that causes unification to
succeed.

```
?- X = a.
X = a

?- 4 = Y.
Y = 4

?- location(apple, kitchen) =
location(apple, X).
```

```
X = kitchen
```

In other cases multiple variables are simultaneously bound to values.

```
?- location(X,Y) = location(apple,
kitchen).
X = apple
Y = kitchen
```

```
?- location(apple, X) = location(Y,
kitchen).
X = kitchen
Y = apple
```

Variables can also unify with each other. Each instance of a variable has a unique internal Prolog value. When two variables are unified to each other, Prolog notes that they must have the same value. In the following example, it is assumed Prolog uses '_nn,' where 'n' is a digit, to represent unbound variables.

```
?- X = Y.
X = _01
Y = _01
```

```
?- location(X, kitchen) = location(Y,
kitchen).
X = _01
Y = _01
```

Prolog remembers the fact that the variables are bound together and will reflect this if either is later bound.

```
?- X = Y, Y = hello.
X = hello
Y = hello
```

```
?- X = Y, a(Z) = a(Y), X = hello.
X = hello
Y = hello
Z = hello
```

The last example is critical to a good understanding of Prolog and illustrates a major difference between unification with Prolog variables and assignment with variables found in most other languages. Note carefully the behavior of the following queries.

```
?- X = Y, Y = 3, write(X).
3
X = 3
Y = 3


?- X = Y, tastes_yucky(X), write(Y).
broccoli
X = broccoli
Y = broccoli
```

When two structures with variables are unified with each other, the variables take on values that make the two structures identical. Note that a structure bound to a variable can itself contain variables.

```
?- X = a(b,c).
X = a(b,c)

?- a(b,X) = a(b,c(d,e)).
X = c(d,e)

?- a(b,X) = a(b,c(Y,e)).
X = c(_01,e)
Y = _01
```

Even in these more complex examples, the relationships between variables are remembered and updated as new variable bindings occur.

```
?- a(b,X) = a(b,c(Y,e)), Y = hello.
X = c(hello, e)
Y = hello


?- food(X,Y) = Z, write(Z), nl,
tastes_yucky(X), edible(Y), write(Z).
```

```
food(_01,_02)
food(broccoli, apple)
X = broccoli
Y = apple
Z = food(broccoli, apple)
```

If a new value assigned to a variable in later goals conflicts with the pattern set earlier, the goal fails.

```
?- a(b,X) = a(b,c(Y,e)), X = hello.
no
```

The second goal failed since there is no value of Y that will allow hello to unify with c(Y,e). The following will succeed.

```
?- a(b,X) = a(b,c(Y,e)), X = c(hello, e).
X = c(hello, e)
Y = hello
```

If there is no possible value the variable can take on, then unification fails.

```
?- a(X) = a(b,c).
no
```

```
?- a(b,c,d) = a(X,X,d).
no
```

The last example failed because the pattern asks that the first two arguments be the same, and they aren't.

```
?- a(c,X,X) = a(Y,Y,b).
no
```

Did you understand why this example fails? Matching the first argument binds Y to c. The second argument causes X and Y to have the same value, in this case c. The third argument asks that X bind to b, but it is already bound to c. No value of X and Y will allow these two structures to unify.

The anonymous variable (_) is a wild variable, and does not bind to values. Multiple occurrences of it do not imply equal values.

```
?- a(c,X,X) = a(_,_,b).
```

```
X = b
```

Unification occurs explicitly when the equal (=) built-in predicate is used, and implicitly when Prolog searches for the head of a clause that matches a goal pattern.

Exercises
Nonsense Prolog

Predict the results of these unification queries.

```
?- a(b,c) = a(X,Y).
```

```
?- a(X,c(d,X)) = a(2,c(d,Y)).
```

```
?- a(X,Y) = a(b(c,Y),Z).
```

```
?- tree(left, root, Right) = tree(left,
root,
   tree(a, b, tree(c, d, e))).
```

11- Lists

Lists are powerful data structures for holding and manipulating groups of things.

In Prolog, a list is simply a collection of terms. The terms can be any Prolog data types, including structures and other lists. Syntactically, a list is denoted by square brackets with the terms separated by commas. For example, a list of things in the kitchen is represented as

```
[apple, broccoli, refrigerator]
```

This gives us an alternative way of representing the locations of things. Rather than having separate location predicates for each thing, we can have one location predicate per container, with a list of things in the container.

```
loc_list([apple, broccoli, crackers],
kitchen).
loc_list([desk, computer], office).
loc_list([flashlight, envelope], desk).
loc_list([stamp, key], envelope).
loc_list(['washing machine'], cellar).
loc_list([nani], 'washing machine').
```

There is a special list, called the empty list, which is represented by a set of empty brackets ([]). It is also referred to as nil. It can describe the lack of contents of a place or thing.

```
loc_list([], hall)
```

Unification works on lists just as it works on other data structures. With what we now know about lists we can ask

```
?- loc_list(X, kitchen).
X = [apple, broccoli, crackers]

?- [_,X,_] = [apples, broccoli, crackers].
X = broccoli
```

This last example is an impractical method of getting at list elements, since the patterns won't unify unless both lists have the same number of elements.

For lists to be useful, there must be easy ways to access, add, and delete list elements. Moreover, we should not have to concern ourselves about the number of list items, or their order.

Two Prolog features enable us to accomplish this easy access. One is a special notation that allows reference to the first element of a list and the list of remaining elements, and the other is recursion.

These two features allow us to write list utility predicates, such as member/2, which finds members of a list, and append/3, which joins two lists together. List predicates all follow a similar strategy —try something with the first element of a list, then recursively repeat the process on the rest of the list.

First, the special notation for list structures.

```
[X | Y]
```

When this structure is unified with a list, X is bound to the first element of the list, called the head. Y is bound to the list of remaining elements, called the tail.

We will now look at some examples of unification using lists. The following example successfully unifies because the two structures are syntactically equivalent. Note that the tail is a list.

```
?- [a|[b,c,d]] = [a,b,c,d].
yes
```

This next example fails because of misuse of the bar (|) symbol. What follows the bar must be a single term, which for all practical purposes must be a list. The example incorrectly has three terms after the bar.

```
?- [a|b,c,d] = [a,b,c,d].
no
```

Here are some more examples.

```
?- [H|T] = [apple, broccoli,
refrigerator].
```

```
H = apple
T = [broccoli, refrigerator]

?- [H|T] = [a, b, c, d, e].
H = a
T = [b, c, d, e]

?- [H|T] = [apples, bananas].
H = apples
T = [bananas]
```

In the previous and following examples, the tail is a list with one element.

```
?- [H|T] = [a, [b,c,d]].
H = a
T = [[b, c, d]]
```

In the next case, the tail is the empty list.

```
?- [H|T] = [apples].
H = apples
T = []
```

The empty list does not unify with the standard list syntax because it has no head.

```
?- [H|T] = [].
no
```

NOTE: This last failure is important, because it is often used to test for the boundary condition in a recursive routine. That is, as long as there are elements in the list, a unification with the [X|Y] pattern will succeed. When there are no elements in the list, that unification fails, indicating that the boundary condition applies.

We can specify more than just the first element before the bar (|). In fact, the only rule is that what follows it should be a list.

```
?- [One, Two | T] = [apple, sprouts,
fridge, milk].
One = apple
Two = sprouts
```

```
T = [fridge, milk]
```

Notice in the next examples how each of the variables is bound to a structure that shows the relationships between the variables. The internal variable numbers indicate how the variables are related. In the first example Z, the tail of the right-hand list, is unified with [Y| T]. In the second example T, the tail of the left-hand list is unified with [Z]. In both cases, Prolog looks for the most general way to relate or bind the variables.

```
?- [X,Y|T] = [a|Z].
X = a
Y = _01
T = _03
Z = [_01 | _03]

?- [H|T] = [apple, Z].
H = apple
T = [_01]
Z = _01
```

Study these last two examples carefully, because list unification is critical in building list utility predicates.

A list can be thought of as a head and a tail list, whose head is the second element and whose tail is a list whose head is the third element, and so on.

```
?- [a|[b|[c|[d|[]]]]] = [a,b,c,d].
yes
```

We have said a list is a special kind of structure. In a sense it is, but in another sense it is just like any other Prolog term. The last example gives us some insight into the true nature of the list. It is really an ordinary two-argument predicate. The first argument is the head and the second is the tail. If we called it dot/2, then the list [a,b,c,d] would be

```
dot(a,dot(b,dot(c,dot(d,[]))))
```

In fact, the predicate does exist, at least conceptually, and it is called dot, but it is represented by a period (.) instead of dot.

To see the dot notation, we use the built-in predicate display/1, which is similar to write/1, except it always uses the dot syntax for lists when it writes to the console.

```
?- X = [a,b,c,d], write(X), nl,
display(X), nl.
   [a,b,c,d]
   .(a,.(b,.(c,.d(,[])))) 

?- X = [Head|Tail], write(X), nl,
display(X), nl.
   [_01, _02]
   .(_01,_02)

?- X = [a,b,[c,d],e], write(X), nl,
display(X), nl.
   [a,b,[c,d],e]
   .(a,.(b,.(.(c,.(d,[])),.(e,[]))))
```

From these examples it should be clear why there is a different syntax for lists. The easier syntax makes for easier reading, but sometimes obscures the behavior of the predicate. It helps to keep this "real" structure of lists in mind when working with predicates that manipulate lists.

This structure of lists is well-suited for the writing of recursive routines. The first one we will look at is member/2, which determines whether or not a term is a member of a list.

As with most recursive predicates, we will start with the boundary condition, or the simple case. An element is a member of a list if it is the head of the list.

```
member(H,[H|T]).
```

This clause also illustrates how a fact with variable arguments acts as a rule.

The second clause of member/2 is the recursive rule. It says an element is a member of a list if it is a member of the tail of the list.

```
member(X,[H|T]) :- member(X,T).
```

The full predicate is

```
member(H,[H|T]).
member(X,[H|T]) :- member(X,T).
```

Note that both clauses of member/2 expect a list as the second argument. Since T in [H|T] in the second clause is itself a list, the recursive call to member/2 works.

```
?- member(apple, [apple, broccoli,
crackers]).
   yes
```

```
?- member(broccoli, [apple, broccoli,
crackers]).
   yes
```

```
?- member(banana, [apple, broccoli,
crackers]).
   no
```

Figure 11.1 has a full annotated trace of member/2.

The query is

```
?- member(b, [a,b,c]).
```

```
1-1 CALL member(b,[a,b,c])
```

The goal pattern fails to unify with the head of the first clause of member/2, because the pattern in the head of the first clause calls for the head of the list and first argument to be identical. The goal pattern can unify with the head of the second clause.

```
1-1 try (2) member(b,[a,b,c])
```

The second clause recursively calls another copy of member/2.

```
   2-1 CALL member(b,[b,c])
```

It succeeds because the call pattern unifies with the
head of the first clause.

```
2-1 EXIT (1) member(b,[b,c])
```

The success ripples back to the outer level.

```
1-1 EXIT (2) member(b,[a,b,c])
    yes
```

Figure 11.1. Trace of member/2

As with many Prolog predicates, member/2 can be used in multiple
ways. If the first argument is a variable, member/2 will, on
backtracking, generate all of the terms in a given list.

```
?- member(X, [apple, broccoli, crackers]).
X = apple ;
X = broccoli ;
X = crackers ;
no
```

We will now trace this use of member/2 using the internal
variables. Remember that each level has its own unique variables,
but that they are tied together based on the unification patterns
between the goal at one level and the head of the clause on the next
level.

In this case the pattern is simple in the recursive clause of member.
The head of the clause unifies X with the first argument of the
original goal, represented by _0 in the following trace. The body
has a call to member/2 in which the first argument is also X,
therefore causing the next level to unify with the same _0. Figure
11.2 has the trace.

The query is

```
?- member(X,[a,b,c]).
```

The goal succeeds by unification with the head of the
first clause, if X = a.

```
1-1 CALL member(_0,[a,b,c])
1-1 EXIT (1) member(a,[a,b,c])
```

```
     X = a ;
```

Backtracking unbinds the variable and the second clause is tried.

```
1-1 REDO member(_0,[a,b,c])
1-1 try (2) member(_0,[a,b,c])
```

It succeeds on the second level, just as on the first level.

```
  2-1 CALL member(_0,[b,c])
  2-1 EXIT (1) member(b,[b,c])
1-1 EXIT  member(b,[a,b,c])
   X = b ;
```

Backtracking continues onto the third level, with similar results.

```
  2-1 REDO member(_0,[b,c])
  2-1 try (2) member(_0,[b,c])
    3-1 CALL member(_0,[c])
    3-1 EXIT (1) member(c,[c])
  2-1 EXIT (2) member(c,[b,c])
1-1 EXIT (2) member(c,[a,b,c])
   X = c ;
```

Further backtracking causes an attempt to find a member of the empty list. The empty list does not unify with either of the list patterns in the member/2 clauses, so the query fails back to the beginning.

```
    3-1 REDO member(_0,[c])
    3-1 try (2) member(_0,[c])
      4-1 CALL member(_0,[])
      4-1 FAIL member(_0,[])
    3-1 FAIL member(_0,[c])
  2-1 FAIL member(_0,[b,c])
1-1 FAIL member(_0,[a,b,c])
   no
```

Figure 11.2. Trace of member/2 generating elements of a list

Another very useful list predicate builds lists from other lists or alternatively splits lists into separate pieces. This predicate is usually called append/3. In this predicate the second argument is

appended to the first argument to yield the third argument. For
example

```
?- append([a,b,c],[d,e,f],X).
X = [a,b,c,d,e,f]
```

It is a little more difficult to follow, since the basic strategy of
working from the head of the list does not fit nicely with the
problem of adding something to the end of a list. append/3 solves
this problem by reducing the first list recursively.

The boundary condition states that if a list X is appended to the
empty list, the resulting list is also X.

```
append([ ],X,X).
```

The recursive condition states that if list X is appended to list [H|
T1], then the head of the new list is also H, and the tail of the new
list is the result of appending X to the tail of the first list.

```
append([H|T1],X,[H|T2]) :-
   append(T1,X,T2).
```

The full predicate is

```
append([ ],X,X).
append([H|T1],X,[H|T2]) :-
   append(T1,X,T2).
```

Real Prolog magic is at work here, which the trace alone does not
reveal. At each level, new variable bindings are built, that are
unified with the variables of the previous level. Specifically, the
third argument in the recursive call to append/3 is the tail of the
third argument in the head of the clause. These variable
relationships are included at each step in the annotated trace shown
in Figure 11.3.

The query is

```
?- append([a,b,c],[d,e,f],X).

1-1 CALL append([a,b,c],[d,e,f],_0)
   X = _0
   2-1 CALL append([b,c],[d,e,f],_5)
      _0 = [a|_5]
```

```
    3-1 CALL append([c],[d,e,f],_9)
    _5 = [b|_9]
    4-1 CALL append([],[d,e,f],_14)
       _9 = [c|_14]
```

By making all the substitutions of the variable
relationships, we can see that at this point X is
bound as follows (thinking in terms of the dot
notation for lists might make append/3 easier to
understand).

X = [a|[b|[c|_14]]]]

We are about to hit the boundary condition, as the
first argument has been reduced to the empty list.
Unifying with the first clause of append/3 will bind
_14 to a value, namely [d,e,f], thus giving us the
desired result for X, as well as all the other
intermediate variables. Notice the bound third
arguments at each level, and compare them to the
variables in the call ports above.

```
    4-1 EXIT (1) append([],[d,e,f],[d,e,f])
    3-1 EXIT (2) append([c],[d,e,f],[c,d,e,f])
  2-1 EXIT (2) append([b,c],[d,e,f],[b,c,d,e,f])
1-1 EXIT (2)append([a,b,c],[d,e,f],[a,b,c,d,e,f])
    X = [a,b,c,d,e,f]
```
Figure 11.3. Trace of append/3

Like member/2, append/3 can also be used in other ways, for
example, to break lists apart as follows.

```
?- append(X,Y,[a,b,c]).
X = []
Y = [a,b,c] ;

X = [a]
Y = [b,c] ;

X = [a,b]
Y = [c] ;
```

```
X = [a,b,c]
Y = [] ;
no
```

Using the List Utilities

Now that we have tools for manipulating lists, we can use them.
For example, if we choose to use loc_list/2 instead of location/2 for
storing things, we can write a new location/2 that behaves exactly
like the old one, except that it computes the answer rather than
looking it up. This illustrates the sometimes fuzzy line between
data and procedure. The rest of the program cannot tell how
location/2 gets its results, whether as data or by computation. In
either case it behaves the same, even on backtracking.

```
location(X,Y):-
    loc_list(List, Y),
    member(X, List).
```

In the game, it will be necessary to add things to the loc_lists
whenever something is put down in a room. We can write
add_thing/3 which uses append/3. If we call it with NewThing and
Container, it will provide us with the NewList.

```
add_thing(NewThing, Container, NewList):-
    loc_list(OldList, Container),
    append([NewThing],OldList, NewList).
```

Testing it gives

```
?- add_thing(plum, kitchen, X).
X = [plum, apple, broccoli, crackers]
```

However, this is a case where the same effect can be achieved
through unification and the [Head|Tail] list notation.

```
add_thing2(NewThing, Container, NewList):-
    loc_list(OldList, Container),
    NewList = [NewThing | OldList].
```

It works the same as the other one.

```
?- add_thing2(plum, kitchen, X).
X = [plum, apple, broccoli, crackers]
```

We can simplify it one step further by removing the explicit unification, and using the implicit unification that occurs at the head of a clause, which is the preferred form for this type of predicate.

```
add_thing3(NewTh, Container,[NewTh|
OldList])  :-
    loc_list(OldList, Container).
```

It also works the same.

```
?- add_thing3(plum, kitchen, X).
X = [plum, apple, broccoli, crackers]
```

In practice, we might write put_thing/2 directly without using the separate add_thing/3 predicate to build a new list for us.

```
put_thing(Thing,Place)  :-
    retract(loc_list(List, Place)),
    asserta(loc_list([Thing|List],Place)).
```

Whether you use multiple database entries or lists for situations, such as we have with locations of things, is largely a matter of style. Your experience will lead you to one or the other in different situations. Sometimes backtracking over multiple predicates is a more natural solution to a problem and sometimes recursively dealing with a list is more natural.

You might find that some parts of a particular application fit better with multiple facts in the database and other parts fit better with lists. In these cases it is useful to know how to go from one format to the other.

Going from a list to multiple facts is simple. You write a recursive routine that continually asserts the head of the list. In this example we create individual facts in the predicate stuff/1.

```
break_out([]).
break_out([Head | Tail]):-
```

```
     assertz(stuff(Head)),
     break_out(Tail).
```
Here's how it works.
```
?- break_out([pencil, cookie, snow]).
yes
```
```
?- stuff(X).
X = pencil ;
X = cookie ;
X = snow ;
no
```
Transforming multiple facts into a list is more difficult. For this reason most Prologs provide built-in predicates that do the job. The most common one is findall/3. The arguments are

arg1	A pattern for the terms in the resulting list
arg2	A goal pattern
arg3	The resulting list

findall/3 automatically does a full backtracking search of the goal pattern and stores each result in the list. It can recover our stuff/1 back into a list.

```
?- findall(X, stuff(X), L).
L = [pencil, cookie, snow]
```
Fancier patterns are available. This is how to get a list of all the rooms connecting to the kitchen.

```
?- findall(X, connect(kitchen, X), L).
L = [office, cellar, 'dining room']
```
The pattern in the first argument can be even fancier and the second argument can be a conjunction of goals. Parentheses are used to group the conjunction of goals in the second argument, thus avoiding the potential ambiguity. Here findall/3 builds a list of structures that locates the edible things.

```
?- findall(foodat(X,Y), (location(X,Y) ,
edible(X)), L).
```

```
L = [foodat(apple, kitchen),
foodat(crackers, kitchen)]
```

Exercises

List Utilities

1- Write list utilities that perform the following functions.

- Remove a given element from a list

- Find the element after a given element

- Split a list into two lists at a given element (Hint - append/3 is close.)

- Get the last element of a list

- Count the elements in a list (Hint - the length of the empty list is 0, the length a non-empty list is 1 + the length of its tail.)

2- Because write/1 only takes a single argument, multiple 'writes' are necessary for writing a mixed string of text and variables. Write a list utility respond/1 which takes as its single argument a list of terms to be written. This can be used in the game to communicate with the player. For example

```
respond(['You can''t get to the', Room,
'from here'])
```

3- Lists with a variable tail are called open lists. They have some interesting properties. For example, member/2 can be used to add items to an open list. Experiment with and trace the following queries.

```
?- member(a,X).
?- member(b, [a,b,c|X]).
?- member(d, [a,b,c|X]).
```

```
?- OpenL = [a,b,c|X], member(d, OpenL),
write(OpenL).
```

Nonsense Prolog

4- Predict the results of the following queries.

```
?- [a,b,c,d] = [H|T].
?- [a,[b,c,d]] = [H|T].
?- [] = [H|T].
?- [a] = [H|T].
?- [apple,3,X,'What?'] = [A,B|Z].
?- [[a,b,c],[d,e,f],[g,h,i]] = [H|T].
?- [a(X,c(d,Y)), b(2,3), c(d,Y)] = [H|T].
```

Genealogical Database

5- Consider the following Prolog program

```
parent(a1,a2).
parent(a2,a3).
parent(a3,a4).
parent(a4,a5).

ancestor(A,D,[A]) :- parent(A,D).
ancestor(A,D,[X|Z]) :-
   parent(X,D),
   ancestor(A,X,Z).
```

6- What is the purpose of the third argument to ancestor?

7- Predict the response to the following queries. Check by tracing in Prolog.

```
?- ancestor(a2,a3,X).
?- ancestor(a1,a5,X).
?- ancestor(a5,a1,X).
?- ancestor(X,a5,Z).
```

Expert System

8- Lists provide a convenient way to provide a simple menu

capability to our expert system. We can replace the 'ask' predicate with menuask/3 where appropriate. menuask/3 will ask the player to select an item from a menu. The format is

```
menuask(Attribute, Value,
List_of_Choices).
```

For example

```
size(X):- menuask(size, X, [large, medium,
small]).
```

This requires two intermediate predicates, menu_display/2 and menu_select/2. The first writes each choice on a separate line preceded by a unique number. The second uses a number entered by the user to return the "nth" element of the list.

12- Operators

We have seen that the form of a Prolog data structure is

```
functor(arg1,arg2,...,argN).
```

This is the ONLY data structure in Prolog. However, Prolog allows for other ways to syntactically represent the same data structure. These other representations are sometimes called syntactic sugaring. The equivalence between list syntax and the dot (.) functor is one example. Operator syntax is another.

Chapter 6 introduced arithmetic operators. In this chapter we will equate them to the standard Prolog data structures, and learn how to define any functor to be an operator.

Each arithmetic operator is an ordinary Prolog functor, such as -/2, +/2, and -/1. The display/1 predicate can be used to see the standard syntax.

```
?- display(2 + 2).
+(2,2)

?- display(3 * 4 + 6).
+(*(3,4),6)

?- display(3 * (4 + 6)).
*(3,+(4,6))
```

You can define any functor to be an operator, in which case the Prolog listener will be able to read the structure in a different format. For example, if location/2 was an operator we could write

```
apple location kitchen.
```

instead of

```
location(apple, kitchen).
```

NOTE: The fact that location is an operator is of NO significance to Prolog's pattern matching. It simply means there is an alternative way of writing the same term.

Operators are of three types.

infix	Example: 3 + 4
prefix	Example: -7
postfix	Example: 8 factorial

They have a number representing precedence which runs from 1 to 1200. When a term with multiple operators is converted to pure syntax, the operators with higher precedences are converted first. A high precedence is indicated by a low number.

Operators are defined with the built-in predicate op/3, whose three arguments are precedence, associativity, and the operator name.

Associativity in the second argument is represented by a pattern that defines the type of operator. The first example we will see is the definition of an infix operator which uses the associativity pattern 'xfx.' The 'f' indicates the position of the operator in respect to its arguments. We will see other patterns as we proceed.

For our current purposes, we will again rework the location/2 predicate and rename it is_in/2 to go with its new look, and we will represent rooms in the structure room/1.

```
is_in(apple, room(kitchen)).
```

We will now make is_in/2 an infix operator of arbitrary precedence 35.

```
?- op(35,xfx,is_in).
```

Now we can ask

```
?- apple is_in X.
X = room(kitchen)
```

or

```
?- X is_in room(kitchen).
X = apple
```

We can add facts to the program in operator syntax.

```
banana is_in room(kitchen).
```

To verify that Prolog treats both syntaxes the same we can attempt to unify them.

```
?- is_in(banana, room(kitchen)) = banana
is_in room(kitchen).
yes
```

And we can use display/1 to look at the new syntax.

```
?- display(banana is_in room(kitchen)).
is_in(banana, room(kitchen))
```

Let's now make room/1 a prefix operator. Note that in this case the associativity pattern fx is used to indicate the functor comes before the argument. Also we chose a precedence (33) higher (higher precedence has lower number) than that used for is_in (35) in order to nest the room structure inside the is_in structure.

?- op(33,fx,room).

Now room/1 is displayed in operator syntax.

```
?- room kitchen = room(kitchen).
yes

?- apple is_in X.
X = room kitchen
```

The operator syntax can be used to add facts to the program.

```
pear is_in room kitchen.

?- is_in(pear, room(kitchen)) = pear is_in
room kitchen.
yes

?- display(pear is_in room kitchen).
is_in(pear, room(kitchen))
```

CAUTION: If you mix up the precedence (easy to do) you will get strange bugs. If room/1 had a lower precedence (higher number) than is_in/2, then the structure would be

```
room(is_in(apple, kitchen))
```

Not only doesn't this capture the information as intended, it also will not unify the way we want.

For completeness, an example of a candidate for a postfix operator would be turned_on. Again note that the 'xf' pattern says that the functor comes after the argument.

```
?- op(33,xf,turned_on).
```

We can now say

```
flashlight turned_on.
```

and

```
?- turned_on(flashlight) = flashlight
turned_on.
    yes
```

Operators are useful for making more readable data structures in a program and for making quick and easy user interfaces.

In our command-driven Nani Search, we use a simple natural language front end, which will be described in the last chapter. We could have alternatively made the commands operators so that

goto(kitchen)	becomes goto kitchen.
turn_on(flashlight)	becomes turn_on flashlight.
take(apple)	becomes take apple.

It's not natural language, but it's a lot better than parentheses and commas.

We have seen how the precedence of operators affects their translation into structures. When operators are of equal precedence, the Prolog reader must decide whether to work from left to right, or right to left. This is the difference between right and left associativity.

An operator can also be non-associative, which means an error is generated if you try to string two together.

The same pattern used for precedence is used for associativity with the additional character y. The options are

Infix	xfx	Non-associative
	xfy	Right to left
	yfx	Left to right
Prefix	fx	Non-associative
	fy	Left to right
Postfix	xf	Non-associative
	yf	Right to left

The is_in/2 predicate is currently non-associative so this gets an error.

```
key is_in desk is_in office.
```

To represent nesting, we would want this to be evaluated from right to left.

```
?- op(35,xfy,is_in).
yes

?- display(key is_in desk is_in office).
is_in(key, is_in(desk, office))
```

If we set it left to right the arguments would be different.

```
?- op(35,yfx,is_in).
yes

?- display(key is_in desk is_in office).
is_in(is_in(key, desk), office)
```

We can override operator associativity and precedence with parentheses. Thus we can get our left to right is_in to behave right to left like so.

```
?- display(key is_in (desk is_in office)).
is_in(key, is_in(desk, office))
```

Many built-in predicates are actually defined as infix operators. That means that rather than following the standard predicate(arg1,arg2) format, the predicate can appear between the arguments as

```
arg1 predicate arg2.
```

The arithmetic operators we have seen already illustrate this. For example +, -, *, and / are used as you would expect. However, it is important to understand that these arithmetic structures are just structures like any others, and do not imply arithmetic evaluation. 3 + 4 is not the same as 7 any more than plus(3,4) is or likes(3,4). It is just +(3,4).

Only special built-in predicates, like is/2, actually perform an arithmetic evaluation of an arithmetic expression. As we have seen, is/2 causes the right side to be evaluated and the left side is unified with the evaluated result.

This is in contrast to the unification (=) predicate, which just unifies terms without evaluating them.

```
?- X is 3 + 4.
X = 7

?- X = 3 + 4.
X = 3 + 4

?- 10 is 5 * 2.
yes

?- 10 = 5 * 2.
no
```

Arithmetic expressions can be as arbitrarily complex as other structures.

```
?- X is 3 * 4 + (6 / 2).
X = 15
```

Even if they are not evaluated.

```
?- X = 3 * 4 + (6 / 2).
X = 3 * 4 + (6 / 2)
```

The operator predicates can also be written in standard notation.

```
?- X is +(*(3,4) , /(6,2)).
X = 15

?- 3 * 4 + (6 / 2) = +(*(3,4),/(6,2)).
yes
```

To underscore that these arithmetic operators are really ordinary predicates with no special meaning unless being evaluated by is/2, consider

```
?- X = 3 * 4 + likes(john, 6/2).
X = 3 * 4 + likes(john, 6/2).

?- X is 3 * 4 + likes(john, 6/2).
error
```

We have seen that Prolog programs are composed of clauses. These clauses are simply Prolog data structures written with operator syntax. The functor is the neck (:-) which is defined as an infix operator. There are two arguments.

```
:-(Head, Body).
```

The body is a data structure with the functor 'and' represented by a comma (,). The body looks like

```
,(goal1, ,(goal2,,goal3))
```

Note the ambiguous use of the comma (,) as a conjunctive operator and as a separator of arguments in a Prolog structure. This can cause confusion in Prolog programs that manipulate Prolog clauses. It might have been clearer if an ampersand (&) was used instead of a comma for separating goals. Then the above pattern would be

```
&(goal1, &(goal2, & goal3))
```

and the following would be equivalent.

```
head :- goal1 & goal2 & goal3.
:-(head, &(goal1, &(goal2, & goal3))).
```

But that is not how it was done, so the two forms are

```
head :- goal1 , goal2 , goal3.
:-(head, ,(goal1, ,(goal2, , goal3))).
```

Every other comma has a different meaning.

The arithmetic operators are often used by Prolog programmers to syntactically join related terms. For example, the write/1 predicate takes only one argument, but operators give an easy way around this restriction.

```
?- X = one, Y = two, write(X-Y).
one - two
```

The slash (/) can be used the same way. In addition, some Prologs define the colon (:) as an operator just for this purpose. It can improve readability by removing some parentheses. For example, the complex structures for defining things in the game can be syntactically represented with the colon as well.

```
object(apple, size:small, color:red,
weight:1).
```

A query looking for small things would be expressed

```
?- object(X, size:small, color:C,
weight:W).
X = apple
C = red
W = 1
```

The pattern matching is the same as always, but instead of size(small) we use the pattern size:small, which is really : (size,small).

Exercises

Adventure Game

1- Define all of the Nani Search commands as operators so the current version of the game can be played without parentheses or commas.

Genealogical Database

2- Define the various relationships in the genealogical database as operators.

13- Cut

Up to this point, we have worked with Prolog's backtracking execution behavior. We have seen how to use that behavior to write compact predicates.

Sometimes it is desirable to selectively turn off backtracking. Prolog provides a predicate that performs this function. It is called the cut, represented by an exclamation point (!).

The cut effectively tells Prolog to freeze all the decisions made so far in this predicate. That is, if required to backtrack, it will automatically fail without trying other alternatives.

We will first examine the effects of the cut and then look at some practical reasons to use it.

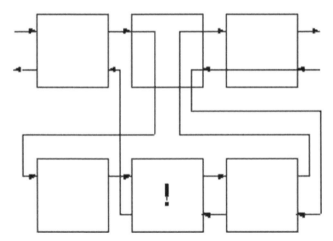

Figure 13.1. The effect of the cut on flow of control

When the cut is encountered, it re-routes backtracking, as shown in figure 13.1. It short-circuits backtracking in the goals to its left on its level, and in the level above, which contained the cut. That is, both the parent goal (middle goal of top level) and the goals of the particular rule being executed (second level) are affected by the cut. The effect is undone if a new route is taken into the parent goal. Contrast figure 13.1 with figure 5.1.

We will write some simple predicates that illustrate the behavior of the cut, first adding some data to backtrack over.

```
data(one).
data(two).
data(three).
```

Here is the first test case. It has no cut and will be used for comparison purposes.

```
cut_test_a(X) :-
   data(X).
cut_test_a('last clause').
```

This is the control case, which exhibits the normal behavior.

```
?- cut_test_a(X), write(X), nl, fail.
one
two
three
last clause
no
```

Next, we put a cut at the end of the first clause.

```
cut_test_b(X) :-
   data(X),
   !.
cut_test_b('last clause').
```

Note that it stops backtracking through both the data/1 subgoal (left), and the cut_test_b parent (above).

```
?- cut_test_b(X), write(X), nl, fail.
one
no
```

Next we put a cut in the middle of two subgoals.

```
cut_test_c(X,Y) :-
   data(X),
   !,
   data(Y).
cut_test_c('last clause').
```

Note that the cut inhibits backtracking in the parent cut_test_c and in the goals to the left of (before) the cut (first data/1). The second data/1 to the right of (after) the cut is still free to backtrack.

```
?- cut_test_c(X,Y), write(X-Y), nl, fail.
one - one
one - two
one - three
no
```

Performance is the main reason to use the cut. This separates the logical purists from the pragmatists. Various arguments can also be made as to its effect on code readability and maintainability. It is often called the 'goto' of logic programming.

You will most often use the cut when you know that at a certain point in a given predicate, Prolog has either found the only answer, or if it hasn't, there is no answer. In this case you insert a cut in the predicate at that point.

Similarly, you will use it when you want to force a predicate to fail in a certain situation, and you don't want it to look any further.

Using the Cut

We will now introduce to the game the little puzzles that make adventure games fun to play. We will put them in a predicate called puzzle/1. The argument to puzzle/1 will be one of the game commands, and puzzle/1 will determine whether or not there are special constraints on that command, reacting accordingly.

We will see examples of both uses of the cut in the puzzle/1 predicate. The behavior we want is

    •   If there is a puzzle, and the constraints are met,
quietly succeed.

    •   If there is a puzzle, and the constraints are not met, noisily fail.

- If there is no puzzle, quietly succeed.

The puzzle in Nani Search is that in order to get to the cellar, the game player needs to both have the flashlight and turn it on. If these criteria are met we know there is no need to ever backtrack through puzzle/1 looking for other clauses to try. For this reason we include the cut.

```
puzzle(goto(cellar)):-
  have(flashlight),
  turned_on(flashlight),
  !.
```

If the puzzle constraints are not met, then let the player know there is a special problem. In this case we also want to force the calling predicate to fail, and we don't want it to succeed by moving to other clauses of puzzle/1. Therefore we use the cut to stop backtracking, and we follow it with fail.

```
puzzle(goto(cellar)):-
  write('It''s dark and you are afraid of
the dark.'),
  !, fail.
```

The final clause is a catchall for those commands that have no special puzzles associated with them. They will always succeed in a call to puzzle/1.

```
puzzle(_).
```

For logical purity, it is always possible to rewrite the predicates without the cut. This is done with the built-in predicate not/1. Some claim this provides for clearer code, but often the explicit and liberal use of 'not' clutters up the code, rather than clarifying it.

When using the cut, the order of the rules becomes important. Our second clause for puzzle/1 safely prints an error message, because we know the only way to get there is by the first clause failing before it reached the cut.

The third clause is completely general, because we know the
earlier clauses have caught the special cases.

If the cuts were removed from the clauses, the second two clauses
would have to be rewritten.

```
puzzle(goto(cellar)):-
  not(have(flashlight)),
  not(turned_on(flashlight)),
  write('Scared of dark message'),
  fail.
puzzle(X):-
  not(X = goto(cellar)).
```

In this case the order of the clauses would not matter.

It is interesting to note that not/1 is defined using the cut. It also
uses call/1, another built-in predicate that calls a predicate.

```
not(X) :- call(X), !, fail.
not(X).
```

In the next chapter we will see how to add a command loop to the
game. Until then we can test the puzzle predicate by including a
call to it in each individual command. For example

```
goto(Place) :-
  puzzle(goto(Place)),
  can_go(Place),
  move(Place),
  look.
```

Assuming the player is in the kitchen, an attempt to go to the cellar
will fail.

```
?- goto(cellar).
```

It's dark and you are afraid of the dark.

```
no

?- goto(office).
You are in the office...
```

Then if the player takes the flashlight, turns it on, and return to the kitchen, all goes well.

```
?- goto(cellar).
You are in the cellar...
```

Exercises
Adventure Game

1- Test the puzzle/1 predicate by setting up various game situations and seeing how it responds. When testing predicates with cuts you should always use the semicolon (;) after each answer to make sure it behaves correctly on backtracking. In our case puzzle/1 should always give one response and fail on backtracking.

2- Add your own puzzles for different situations and commands.

Expert System

3- Modify the ask and menuask predicates to use cut to replace the use of not.

Customer Order Entry

4- Modify the good_customer rules to use cut to prevent the search of other cases once we know one has been found.

14- Control Structures

We have examined the manner in which Prolog interprets goals and have also seen examples of how to manipulate Prolog's execution behavior.

In this chapter we will further explore the control structures you can implement in Prolog and draw parallels between them and the control structures found in more conventional programming languages.

You have already used the combination of fail and write/1 to generate lists of things for the game. This control structure is similar to 'do while' found in most languages.

We will now introduce another built-in predicate that allows us to capitalize on failure. It is repeat/0. It always succeeds the first time it is called, and it always succeeds on backtracking. In other words, you can not backtrack through a repeat/0. It always restarts forward execution.

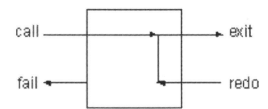

Figure 14.1. Flow of control in the repeat/0 built-in predicate

A clause body with a repeat/0 followed by fail/0 will go back and forth forever. This is one way to write an endless loop in Prolog.

A repeat/0 followed by some intermediate goals followed by a test condition will loop until the test condition is satisfied. It is equivalent to a 'do until' in other languages. This is exactly the behavior we want for the highest command loop in Nani Search.

Our first version of command_loop/0 will simply read commands and echo them until end is entered. The built-in predicate read/1 reads a Prolog term from the console. The term must be followed by a period.

```
command_loop:-
  repeat,
  write('Enter command (end to exit): '),
  read(X),
  write(X), nl,
  X = end.
```

The last goal will fail unless end is entered. The repeat/0 always succeeds on backtracking and causes the intermediate goals to be re-executed.

We can execute it by entering this query.

```
?- command_loop.
```

Now that the control structure is in place, we can have it execute the command, rather than just repeat it.

We will write a new predicate called do/1, which executes only the commands we allow. Many other languages have 'do case' control structures that perform this kind of function. Multiple clauses in a Prolog predicate behave similarly to a 'do case.'

Here is do/1. Notice that it allows us to define synonyms for commands, that is, the player can enter either goto(X) or go(X) to cause the goto/1 predicate to be executed.

```
do(goto(X)):-goto(X),!.
do(go(X)):-goto(X),!.
do(inventory):-inventory,!.
do(look):-look,!.
```

NOTE: The cut serves two purposes. First, it says once we have found a 'do' clause to execute, don't bother looking for anymore. Second, it prevents the backtracking initiated at the end of command_loop from entering the other command predicates.

Here are some more do/1's. If do(end) did not always succeed, we would never get to the' X = end' test and would fail forever. The last do/1 allows us to tell the user there was something wrong with the command.

```
do(take(X)) :- take(X), !.
do(end).
do(_) :-
  write('Invalid command').
```

We can now rewrite command_loop/0 to use the new do/1 and incorporate puzzle/1 in the command loop. We will also replace the old simple test for end with a new predicate, end_condition/1, that will determine if the game is over.

```
command_loop:-
  write('Welcome to Nani Search'), nl,
  repeat,
  write('>nani> '),
  read(X),
  puzzle(X),
  do(X), nl,
  end_condition(X).
```

Two conditions might end the game. The first is if the player types 'end.' The second is if the player has successfully taken the Nani.

```
end_condition(end).
end_condition(_) :-
  have(nani),
  write('Congratulations').
```

The game can now be played from the top.

```
?- command_loop.

Welcome to ...
```

Recursive Control Loop

As hinted at in chapter 7, the purity of logic programming is undermined by the asserts and retracts of the database. Just like global data in any language, predicates that are dynamically asserted and retracted can make for unpredictable code. That is, code in one part of the system that uses a dynamic predicate is affected by code in an entirely different part that changes that dynamic predicate.

For example, puzzle(goto(cellar)) succeeds or fails based on the existence of turned_on(flashlight) which is asserted by the turn_on/1 predicate. A bug in turn_on/1 will cause puzzle/1 to behave incorrectly.

The entire game can be reconstructed using arguments and no global data. To do this, it helps to think of the game as a sequence of state transformations.

In the current implementation, the state of the game is defined by the dynamic predicates location/2, here/1, have/1, and turned_on/1 or turned_off/1 for the flashlight. These predicates define an initial state which is dynamically changed, using assert and retract, as the player moves through the game toward the winning state, which is defined by the existence of have(nani).

We can get the same effect by defining a complex structure to hold the state, implementing game commands that access that state as an argument, rather than from the dynamic database.

Because logical variables cannot have their values changed by assignment, the commands must take two arguments representing the old state and the new state. The repeat-fail control structure will not let us repeatedly change the state in this manner, so we need to write a recursive control structure that recursively sends the new state to itself. The boundary condition is reaching the ending state of the game. This control structure is shown in figure 14.1, which contains an abbreviated version of Nani Search.

The state is represented by a list of structures holding different types of state information, as seen in initial_state/1. The various commands in this type of game need to access and manipulate that state structure. Rather than require each predicate that accesses the state to understand its complex structure, the utility predicates get_state/3, add_state/4, and del_state/4 are written to access it. This way any program changes to the state structure only require changes to the utility predicates.

This style of Prolog programming is logically purer, and lends itself to certain types of applications. It also avoids the difficulties often associated with global data. On the other hand, it requires more complexity in dealing with state information in arguments, and the multiple lists and recursive routines can be confusing to debug. You will have to decide which approach to use for each application you write.

```
/* a nonassertive version of nani search */

nani :-
  write('Welcome to Nani Search'),
  nl,
  initial_state(State),
  control_loop(State).

control_loop(State) :-
  end_condition(State).
control_loop(State) :-
  repeat,
  write('> '),
  read(X),
  constraint(State, X),
  do(State, NewState, X),
  control_loop(NewState).

/* initial dynamic state */

initial_state([
  here(kitchen),
  have([]),
  location([
    kitchen/apple,
    kitchen/broccoli,
    office/desk,
    office/flashlight,
    cellar/nani ]),
status([
  flashlight/off,
  game/on]) ]).

/* static state */
```

```prolog
rooms([office, kitchen, cellar]).

doors([office/kitchen, cellar/kitchen]).

connect(X,Y) :-
  doors(DoorList),
  member(X/Y, DoorList).
connect(X,Y) :-
  doors(DoorList),
  member(Y/X, DoorList).

/* list utilities */

member(X,[X|Y]).
member(X,[Y|Z]) :- member(X,Z).

delete(X, [], []).
delete(X, [X|T], T).
delete(X, [H|T], [H|Z]) :- delete(X, T, Z).

/* state manipulation utilities */

get_state(State, here, X) :-
  member(here(X), State).
get_state(State, have, X) :-
  member(have(Haves), State),
  member(X, Haves).
get_state(State, location, Loc/X) :-
  member(location(Locs), State),
  member(Loc/X, Locs).
get_state(State, status, Thing/Stat) :-
  member(status(Stats), State),
  member(Thing/Stat, Stats).

del_state(OldState, [location(NewLocs) | Temp],
location, Loc/X):-
  delete(location(Locs), OldState, Temp),
  delete(Loc/X, Locs, NewLocs).

add_state(OldState, [here(X)|Temp], here, X) :-
  delete(here(_), OldState, Temp).
add_state(OldState, [have([X|Haves])|Temp], have,
X) :-
  delete(have(Haves), OldState, Temp).
```

```
add_state(OldState, [status([Thing/Stat|TempStats])|
Temp],
status, Thing/Stat) :-
  delete(status(Stats), OldState, Temp),
  delete(Thing/_, Stats, TempStats).


/* end condition */

end_condition(State) :-
  get_state(State, have, nani),
  write('You win').
end_condition(State) :-
  get_state(State, status, game/off),
  write('quitter').


/* constraints and puzzles together */

constraint(State, goto(cellar)) :-
  !, can_go_cellar(State).
constraint(State, goto(X)) :-
  !, can_go(State, X).
constraint(State, take(X)) :-
  !, can_take(State, X).
constraint(State, turn_on(X)) :-
  !, can_turn_on(State, X).
constraint(_, _).

can_go(State,X) :-
  get_state(State, here, H),
  connect(X,H).
can_go(_, X) :-
  write('You can''t get there from here'),
  nl, fail.


can_go_cellar(State) :-
  can_go(State, cellar),
  !, cellar_puzzle(State).


cellar_puzzle(State) :-
  get_state(State, have, flashlight),
  get_state(State, status, flashlight/on).
cellar_puzzle(_) :-
  write('It''s dark in the cellar'),
  nl, fail.
```

```
can_take(State, X) :-
  get_state(State, here, H),
  get_state(State, location, H/X).
can_take(State, X) :-
  write('it is not here'),
  nl, fail.

can_turn_on(State, X) :-
  get_state(State, have, X).
can_turn_on(_, X) :-
  write('You don''t have it'),
  nl, fail.

/* commands */

do(Old, New, goto(X)) :- goto(Old, New, X), !.
do(Old, New, take(X)) :- take(Old, New, X), !.
do(Old, New, turn_on(X)) :- turn_on(Old, New, X), !.
do(State, State, look) :- look(State), !.
do(Old, New, quit) :- quit(Old, New).
do(State, State, _) :-
  write('illegal command'), nl.

look(State) :-
  get_state(State, here, H),
  write('You are in '), write(H),
  nl,
  list_things(State, H), nl.

list_things(State, H) :-
  get_state(State, location, H/X),
  tab(2), write(X),
  fail.
list_things(_, _).

goto(Old, New, X) :-
  add_state(Old, New, here, X),
  look(New).

take(Old, New, X) :-
  get_state(Old, here, H),
  del_state(Old, Temp, location, H/X),
  add_state(Temp, New, have, X).

turn_on(Old, New, X) :-
```

```
  add_state(Old, New, status, X/on).

quit(Old, New) :-
  add_state(Old, New, status, game/off).
```
Figure 14.1. Nani Search without a dynamic database

There could be serious performance problems with this approach to the game. Prolog uses a stack to keep track of the levels of predicate calls. In the case of a recursive predicate, the stack grows at each recursive call. In this example, with its complex arguments, the stack could easily be consumed in a short period of time by the recursive control structure.

Fortunately, there is a performance feature built into Prolog that makes this example program, and ones similar to it, behave efficiently.

Tail Recursion

There are actually two kinds of recursive routines. In a true recursive routine, each level must wait for the information from the lower levels in order to return an answer. This means that Prolog must build a stack with a new entry for each level.

This is in contrast to iteration, which is more common in conventional languages. Each pass through the iteration updates the variables and there is no need for building a stack.

There is a type of recursion called tail recursion that, while written recursively, behaves iteratively. In general, if the recursive call is the last call, and there are no computations based on the information from the lower levels, then a good Prolog can implement the predicate iteratively, without growing the stack.

One classic example of tail recursion is the factorial predicate. First we'll write it using normal recursion. Note that the variable

FF, which is returned from the lower level, is used in the top level.

```
factorial_1(1,1).
factorial_1(N,F):-
  N > 1,
  NN is N - 1,
  factorial_1(NN,FF),
  F is N * FF.
```

It works as expected.

```
?- factorial_1(5,X).
X = 120
```

By introducing a new second argument to keep track of the result so far, we can rewrite factorial/3 tail-recursively. The new argument is initially set to 1. Each recursive call builds on the second argument. When the boundary condition is reached, the third argument is bound to the second argument.

```
factorial_2(1,F,F).
factorial_2(N,T,F):-
  N > 1,
  TT is N * T,
  NN is N - 1,
  factorial_2(NN,TT,F).
```

It gives the same results as the previous version, but because the recursive call is the last call in the second clause, its arguments are not needed at each level.

```
?- factorial_2(5,1,X).
X = 120
```

Another classic example of tail recursion is the predicate to reverse a list. The straightforward definition of 'reverse' would be

```
naive_reverse([],[]).
naive_reverse([H|T],Rev):-
  naive_reverse(T,TR),
  append(TR,[H],Rev).
```

The inefficiency of this definition is a feature taken advantage of in Prolog benchmarks. It is called the naive reverse, and published performance statistics often list the time required to reverse a list of a certain size.

The result of the recursive call to naive_reverse/2 is used in the last goal, so it is not tail recursive, but it gives the right answers.

```
?- naive_reverse([ants, mice, zebras], X).
X = [zebras, mice, ants]
```

By again introducing a new second argument which will accumulate the partial answer through levels of recursion, we can rewrite 'reverse.' It turns out that the partial answer is already reversed when it reaches the boundary condition.

```
reverse([], Rev, Rev).
reverse([H|T], Temp, Rev) :-
   reverse(T, [H|Temp], Rev).
```

We can now try the second reverse.

```
?- reverse([ants, mice, zebras], [], X).
X = [zebras, mice, ants]
```

Exercises

1- Trace both versions of reverse to understand the performance differences.

2- Write a tail recursive predicate that will compute the sum of the numbers between two given numbers. Trace its behavior to see if it is tail recursive.

Adventure Game

3- Add the remaining command predicates to do/1 so the game can be fully played.

4- Add the concept of time to the game by putting a counter in the command loop. Use an out-of-time condition as one way to end the game. Also add a 'wait' command, which just waits for one time increment.

5- Add other individuals or creatures that move automatically through the game rooms. Each cycle of the command loop will update their locations based on whatever algorithm you choose.

Customer Order Entry

6- Write a command loop for the order entry inventory system. Write a variation on menuask/3 that will present the user with a menu of choices, one of which is to exit the system. Use this in the command loop instead of just prompting for a command. Have each command prompt for the required input, if any.

Expert System

7- Make a new version of the expert system that maintains the 'known' information in arguments rather than in the database.

15- Natural Language

Prolog is especially well-suited for developing natural language systems. In this chapter we will create an English front end for Nani Search.

But before moving to Nani Search, we will develop a natural language parser for a simple subset of English. Once that is understood, we will use the same technology for Nani Search.

The simple subset of English will include sentences such as

- The dog ate the bone.

- The big brown mouse chases a lazy cat.

This grammar can be described with the following grammar rules. (The first rule says a sentence is made up of a noun phrase followed by a verb phrase. The last rule says an adjective is either 'big', or 'brown', or 'lazy.' The 'l' means 'or.')

sentence :	nounphrase, verbphrase.
nounphrase :	determiner, nounexpression.
nounphrase :	nounexpression.
nounexpression :	noun.
nounexpression :	adjective, nounexpression.
verbphrase :	verb, nounphrase.
determiner :	the l a.
noun :	dog l bone l mouse l cat.
verb :	ate l chases.
adjective :	big l brown l lazy.

To begin with, we will simply determine if a sentence is a legal sentence. In other words, we will write a predicate sentence/1, which will determine if its argument is a sentence.

The sentence will be represented as a list of words. Our two examples are

```
[the,dog,ate,the,bone]
[the,big,brown,mouse,chases,a,lazy,cat]
```

There are two basic strategies for solving a parsing problem like this. The first is a generate-and-test strategy, where the list to be parsed is split in different ways, with the splittings tested to see if they are components of a legal sentence. We have already seen that we can use append/3 to generate the splittings of a list. With this approach, the top-level rule would be

```
sentence(L) :-
   append(NP, VP, L),
   nounphrase(NP),
   verbphrase(VP).
```

The append/3 predicate will generate possible values for the variables NP and VP, by splitting the original list L. The next two goals test each of the portions of the list to see if they are grammatically correct. If not, backtracking into append/3 causes another possible splitting to be generated.

The clauses for nounphrase/1 and verbphrase/1 are similar to sentence/1, and call further predicates that deal with smaller units of a sentence, until the word definitions are met, such as

```
verb([ate]).
verb([chases]).

noun([mouse]).
noun([dog]).
```

Difference Lists

The above strategy, however, is extremely slow because of the constant generation and testing of trial solutions that do not work. Furthermore, the generating and testing is happening at multiple levels.

The more efficient strategy is to skip the generation step and pass the entire list to the lower level predicates, which in turn will take the grammatical portion of the sentence they are looking for from the front of the list and return the remainder of the list.

To do this, we use a structure called a difference list. It is two related lists, in which the first list is the full list and the second list is the remainder. The two lists can be two arguments in a predicate, but they are more readable if represented as a single argument with the minus sign (-) operator, like X-Y.

Here then is the first grammar rule using difference lists. A list S is a sentence if we can extract a nounphrase from the beginning of it, with a remainder list of S1, and if we can extract a verb phrase from S1 with the empty list as the remainder.

```
sentence(S) :-
   nounphrase(S-S1),
   verbphrase(S1-[]).
```

Before filling in nounphrase/1 and verbphrase/1, we will jump to the lowest level predicates that define the actual words. They too must be difference lists. They are simple. If the head of the first list is the word, the remainder list is simply the tail.

```
noun([dog|X]-X).
noun([cat|X]-X).
noun([mouse|X]-X).

verb([ate|X]-X).
verb([chases|X]-X).

adjective([big|X]-X).
adjective([brown|X]-X).
adjective([lazy|X]-X).
```

```
determiner([the|X]-X).
determiner([a|X]-X).
```

Testing shows how the difference lists work.

```
?- noun([dog,ate,the,bone]-X).
X = [ate,the,bone]

?- verb([dog,ate,the,bone]-X).
no
```

Continuing with the new grammar rules we have

```
nounphrase(NP-X):-
  determiner(NP-S1),
  nounexpression(S1-X).
nounphrase(NP-X):-
  nounexpression(NP-X).

nounexpression(NE-X):-
  noun(NE-X).
nounexpression(NE-X):-
  adjective(NE-S1),
  nounexpression(S1-X).

verbphrase(VP-X):-
  verb(VP-S1),
  nounphrase(S1-X).
```

NOTE: The recursive call in the definition of nounexpression/1. It allows sentences to have any number of adjectives before a noun.

These rules can now be used to test sentences.

```
?- sentence([the,lazy,mouse,ate,a,dog]).
yes

?- sentence([the,dog,ate]).
no

?-
sentence([a,big,brown,cat,chases,a,lazy,brow
```

n,dog]).
   yes

   ?- sentence([the,cat,jumps,the,mouse]).
   no

Figure 15.1 contains a trace of the sentence/1 predicate for a simple sentence.

The query is

```
?- sentence([dog,chases,cat]).

1-1 CALL sentence([dog,chases,cat])
   2-1 CALL nounphrase([dog,chases,cat]-_0)
      3-1 CALL determiner([dog,chases,cat]-_0)
      3-1 FAIL determiner([dog,chases,cat]-_0)
   2-1 REDO nounphrase([dog,chases,cat]-_0)
      3-1 CALL nounexpression([dog,chases,cat]- _0)
         4-1 CALL noun([dog,chases,cat]-_0)
         4-1 EXIT noun([dog,chases,cat]-[chases,cat])
```

Notice how the binding of the variable representing the remainder list has been deferred until the lowest level is called. Each level unifies its remainder with the level before it, so when the vocabulary level is reached, the binding of the remainder to the tail of the list is propagated back up through the nested calls.

```
      3-1 EXIT nounexpression([dog,chases,cat]-
               [chases,cat])
   2-1 EXIT nounphrase([dog,chases,cat]-
            [chases,cat])
```

Now that we have the noun phrase, we can see if the remainder is a verb phrase.

```
   2-2 CALL verbphrase([chases,cat]-[])
      3-1 CALL verb([chases,cat]-_4)
      3-1 EXIT verb([chases,cat]-[cat])
```

Finding the verb was easy, now for the final noun phrase.

```
    3-2 CALL nounphrase([cat]-[])
      4-1 CALL determiner([cat]-[])
      4-1 FAIL determiner([cat]-[])
    3-2 REDO nounphrase([cat]-[])
      4-1 CALL nounexpression([cat]-[])
        5-1 CALL noun([cat]-[])
        5-1 EXIT noun([cat]-[])
      4-1 EXIT nounexpression([cat]-[])
    3-2 EXIT nounphrase([cat]-[])
  2-2 EXIT verbphrase([chases,cat]-[])
1-1 EXIT sentence([dog,chases,cat])
    yes
```

Figure 15.1. Trace of sentence/1

Natural Language Front End

We will now use this sentence-parsing technique to build a simple English language front end for Nani Search.

For the time being we will make two assumptions. The first is that we can get the user's input sentence in list form. The second is that we can represent our commands in list form. For example, we can express goto(office) as [goto, office], and look as [look].

With these assumptions, the task of our natural language front end is to translate a user's natural sentence list into an acceptable command list. For example, we would want to translate [go,to,the,office] into [goto, office].

We will write a high-level predicate, called command/2, that performs this translation. Its format will be

```
command(OutputList, InputList).
```

The simplest commands are the ones that are made up of a verb with no object, such as look, list_possessions, and end. We can define this situation as follows.

```
command([V], InList):- verb(V, InList-[]).
```

We will define verbs as in the earlier example, only this time we will include an extra argument, which identifies the command for use in building the output list. We can also allow as many different ways of expressing a command as we feel like as in the two ways to say 'look' and the three ways to say 'end.'

```
verb(look, [look|X]-X).
verb(look, [look,around|X]-X).
verb(list_possessions, [inventory|X]-X).
verb(end, [end|X]-X).
verb(end, [quit|X]-X).
verb(end, [good,bye|X]-X).
```

We can now test what we've got.

```
?- command(X,[look]).
X = [look]

?- command(X,[look,around]).
X = [look]

?- command(X,[inventory]).
X = [list_possessions]

?- command(X,[good,bye]).
X = [end]
```

We now move to the more complicated case of a command composed of a verb and an object. Using the grammatical constructs we saw in the beginning of this chapter, we could easily construct this grammar. However, we would like to have our interface recognize the semantics of the sentence as well as the formal grammar.

For example, we would like to make sure that 'goto' verbs have a place as an object, and that the other verbs have a thing as an object. We can include this knowledge in our natural language routine with another argument.

Here is how the extra argument is used to ensure the object type required by the verb matches the object type of the noun.

```
command([V,O], InList) :-
   verb(Object_Type, V, InList-S1),
   object(Object_Type, O, S1-[]).
```

Here is how we specify the new verbs.

```
verb(place, goto, [go,to|X]-X).
verb(place, goto, [go|X]-X).
verb(place, goto, [move,to|X]-X).
```

We can even recognize the case where the 'goto' verb was implied, that is if the user just typed in a room name without a preceding verb. In this case the list and its remainder are the same. The existing room/1 predicate is used to check if the list element is a room except when the room name is made up of two words.

The rule states "If we are looking for a verb at the beginning of a list, and the list begins with a room, then assume a 'goto' verb was found and return the full list for processing as the object of the 'goto' verb."

```
verb(place, goto, [X|Y]-[X|Y]):- room(X).
verb(place, goto, [dining,room|Y]-
[dining,room|Y]).
```

Some of the verbs for things are

```
verb(thing, take, [take|X]-X).
verb(thing, drop, [drop|X]-X).
verb(thing, drop, [put|X]-X).
verb(thing, turn_on, [turn,on|X]-X).
```

Optionally, an 'object' may be preceded by a determiner. Here are the two rules for 'object,' which cover both cases.

```
object(Type, N, S1-S3) :-
   det(S1-S2),
   noun(Type, N, S2-S3).
object(Type, N, S1-S2) :-
   noun(Type, N, S1-S2).
```

Since we are just going to throw the determiner away, we don't need to carry extra arguments.

```
det([the|X]- X).
det([a|X]-X).
det([an|X]-X).
```

We define nouns like verbs, but use their occurrence in the game to define most of them. Only those names that are made up of two or more words require special treatment. Nouns of place are defined in the game as rooms.

```
noun(place, R, [R|X]-X):- room(R).
noun(place, 'dining room', [dining,room|
X]-X).
```

Things are distinguished by appearing in a 'location' or 'have' predicate. Again, we make exceptions for cases where the thing name has two words.

```
noun(thing, T, [T|X]-X):- location(T,_).
noun(thing, T, [T|X]-X):- have(T).
noun(thing, 'washing machine',
[washing,machine|X]-X).
```

We can build into the grammar an awareness of the current game situation, and have the parser respond accordingly. For example, we might provide a command that allows the player to turn the room lights on or off. This command might be turn_on(light) as opposed to turn_on(flashlight). If the user types in 'turn on the light' we would like to determine which light was meant.

We can assume the room light was always meant, unless the player has the flashlight. In that case we will assume the flashlight was meant.

```
noun(thing, flashlight, [light|X], X):-
have(flashlight).
noun(thing, light, [light|X], X).
```

We can now try it out.

```
?- command(X,[go,to,the,office]).
X = [goto, office]

?- command(X,[go,dining,room]).
```

```
X = [goto, 'dining room']

?- command(X,[kitchen]).
X = [goto, kitchen]

?- command(X,[take,the,apple]).
X = [take, apple]

?- command(X,[turn,on,the,light]).
X = [turn_on, light]

?- asserta(have(flashlight)), command(X,
[turn,on,the,light]).
X = [turn_on, flashlight]
```

It should fail in the following situations that don't conform to our grammar or semantics.

```
?- command(X,[go,to,the,desk]).
no

?- command(X,[go,attic]).
no

?- command(X,[drop,an,office]).
no
```

Definite Clause Grammar

The use of difference lists for parsing is so common in Prolog, that most Prologs contain additional syntactic sugaring that simplifies the syntax by hiding the difference lists from view. This syntax is called Definite Clause Grammar (DCG), and looks like normal Prolog, only the neck symbol (:-) is replaced with an arrow (-->). The DCG representation is parsed and translated to normal Prolog with difference lists.

Using DCG, the 'sentence' predicate developed earlier would be phrased

```
sentence --> nounphrase, verbphrase.
```

This would be translated into normal Prolog, with difference lists, but represented as separate arguments rather than as single arguments separated by a minus (-) as we implemented them. The above example would be translated into the following equivalent Prolog.

```
sentence(S1, S2):-
  nounphrase(S1, S3),
  verbphrase(S3, S2).
```

Thus, if we define 'sentence' using DCG we still must call it with two arguments, even though the arguments were not explicitly stated in the DCG representation.

```
?- sentence([dog,chases,cat], []).
```

The DCG vocabulary is represented by simple lists.

```
noun --> [dog].
verb --> [chases].
```

These are translated into Prolog as difference lists.

```
noun([dog|X], X).
verb([chases|X], X).
```

As with the natural language front end for Nani Search, we often want to mix pure Prolog with the grammar and include extra arguments to carry semantic information. The arguments are simply added as normal arguments and the pure Prolog is enclosed in curly brackets ({}) to prevent the DCG parser from translating it. Some of the complex rules in our game grammar would then be

```
command([V,O]) -->
  verb(Object_Type, V),
  object(Object_Type, O).

verb(place, goto) --> [go, to].
verb(thing, take) --> [take].
```

```
object(Type, N) --> det, noun(Type, N).
object(Type, N) --> noun(Type, N).

det --> [the].
det --> [a].

noun(place,X) --> [X], {room(X)}.
noun(place,'dining room') --> [dining,
room].
noun(thing,X) --> [X], {location(X,_)}.
```

Because the DCG automatically takes off the first argument, we cannot examine it and send it along as we did in testing for a 'goto' verb when only the room name was given in the command. We can recognize this case with an additional 'command' clause.

```
command([goto, Place]) --> noun(place,
Place).
```

Reading Sentences

Now for the missing pieces. We must include a predicate that reads a normal sentence from the user and puts it into a list. Figure 15.2 contains a program to perform the task. It is composed of two parts. The first part reads a line of ASCII characters from the user, using the built-in predicate get0/1, which reads a single ASCII character. The line is assumed terminated by an ASCII 13, which is a carriage return. The second part uses DCG to parse the list of characters into a list of words, using another built-in predicate name/2, which converts a list of ASCII characters into an atom.

```
% read a line of words from the user

read_list(L) :-
   write('> '),
   read_line(CL),
   wordlist(L,CL,[]), !.

read_line(L) :-
   get0(C),
```

```
  buildlist(C,L).

buildlist(13,[]) :- !.
buildlist(C,[C|X]) :-
  get0(C2),
  buildlist(C2,X).

wordlist([X|Y]) --> word(X), whitespace, wordlist(Y).
wordlist([X]) --> whitespace, wordlist(X).
wordlist([X]) --> word(X).
wordlist([X]) --> word(X), whitespace.

word(W) --> charlist(X), {name(W,X)}.

charlist([X|Y]) --> chr(X), charlist(Y).
charlist([X]) --> chr(X).

chr(X) --> [X],{X>=48}.

whitespace --> whsp, whitespace.
whitespace --> whsp.

whsp --> [X], {X<48}.
```

Figure 15.2. Program to read input sentences

The other missing piece converts a command in the format [goto,office] to a normal-looking command goto(office). This is done with a standard built-in predicate called 'univ', which is represented by an equal sign and two periods (=..). It translates a predicate and its arguments into a list whose first element is the predicate name and whose remaining elements are the arguments. It works in reverse as well, which is how we will want to use it. For example

```
?- pred(arg1,arg2) =..  X.
X = [pred, arg1, arg2]

?- pred =..  X.
X = [pred]

?- X =..  [pred,arg1,arg1].
X = pred(arg1, arg2)
```

```
?- X =..  [pred].
X = pred
```

We can now use these two predicates, along with command/2 to write get_command/1, which reads a sentence from the user and returns a command to command_loop/0.

```
get_command(C)  :-
   read_list(L),
   command(CL,L),
   C =..  CL,  !.
get_command(_)  :-
   write('I don''t understand'), nl, fail.
```

We have now gone from writing the simple facts in the early chapters to a full adventure game with a natural language front end. You have also written an expert system, an intelligent genealogical database and a standard business application. Use these as a basis for continued learning by experimentation.

Exercises
Adventure Game

1- Expand the natural language capabilities to handle all of the commands of Nani Search.

2- Expand the natural language front end to allow for compound sentences, such as "go to the kitchen and take the apple," or "take the apple and the broccoli."

3- Expand the natural language to allow for pronouns. To do this the 'noun' predicate must save the last noun and its type. When the word 'it' is encountered pick up that last noun. Then 'take the apple' followed by 'eat it' will work. (You will probably have to go directly to the difference list notation to make sentences such as "turn it on" work.)

Genealogical Database

4- Build a natural language query system that responds to queries such as "Who are dennis' children?" and "How many nephews does jay have?" Assuming you write a predicate get_query/1 that returns a Prolog query, you can call the Prolog query with the call/1 built-in predicate. For example,

```
main_loop :-
  repeat,
  get_query(X),
  call(X),
  X = end.
```

Appendix

This appendix contains sample versions of the four programs described in the book. These are the adventure game (Nani Search), the intelligent genealogical database (Family), the customer order entry system (Custord), and the expert system (Birds).

Nani Search

```
% NANI SEARCH - A sample adventure game


% Nani Search is designed to illustrate Prolog
programming.  It
% is an implementation of the principle example used
in
% APT - The Active Prolog Tutor.

main:- nani_search.        % main entry point

nani_search:-
  init_dynamic_facts,      % predicates which are not
compiled

  write('NANI SEARCH - A Sample Adventure Game'),nl,
  write('Copyright (C) Amzi! inc. 1990-1995'),nl,
  write('No rights reserved, use it as you wish'),nl,
  nl,
  write('Nani Search is designed to illustrate Prolog
programming.'),nl,
  write('As such, it might be the simplest adventure
game.  The game'),nl,
  write('is the primary example used in APT - The
Active Prolog'),nl,
  write('Tutor.  Full source is included as
well.'),nl,
  nl,
  write('Your persona as the adventurer is that of a
three year'),nl,
  write('old.  The Nani is your security blanket.  It
is getting'),nl,
  write('late and you''re tired, but you can''t go to
sleep'),nl,
  write('without your Nani.  Your mission is to find
the Nani.'),nl,
  nl,
  write('You control the game by using simple English
commands'),nl,
  write('expressing the action you wish to take.  You
can go to'),nl,
  write('other rooms, look at your surroundings, look
```

```
in things'),nl,
  write('take things, drop things, eat things,
inventory the'),nl,
  write('things you have, and turn things on and
off.'),nl,
  nl,
  write('Hit any key to continue.'),get0(_),
  write('Type "help" if you need more help on
mechanics.'),nl,
  write('Type "hint" if you want a big hint.'),nl,
  write('Type "quit" if you give up.'),nl,
  nl,
  write('Enjoy the hunt.'),nl,

  look,                    % give a look before
starting the game
  command_loop.

% command_loop - repeats until either the nani is
found or the
%      player types quit

command_loop:-
  repeat,
  get_command(X),
  do(X),
  (nanifound; X == quit).

% do - matches the input command with the predicate
which carries out
%      the command.  More general approaches which
might work in the
%      listener are not supported in the compiler.
This approach
%      also gives tighter control over the allowable
commands.

%      The cuts prevent the forced failure at the end
of "command_loop"
%      from backtracking into the command predicates.

do(goto(X)):-goto(X),!.
do(nshelp):-nshelp,!.
do(hint):-hint,!.
do(inventory):-inventory,!.
```

```
do(take(X)):-take(X),!.
do(drop(X)):-drop(X),!.
do(eat(X)):-eat(X),!.
do(look):-look,!.
do(turn_on(X)):-turn_on(X),!.
do(turn_off(X)):-turn_off(X),!.
do(look_in(X)):-look_in(X),!.
do(quit):-quit,!.

% These are the predicates which control exit from
the game.  If
% the player has taken the nani, then the call to
"have(nani)" will
% succeed and the command_loop will complete.
Otherwise it fails
% and command_loop will repeat.

nanifound:-
  have(nani),
  write('Congratulations, you saved the Nani.'),nl,
  write('Now you can rest secure.'),nl,nl.

quit:-
  write('Giving up?  It''s going to be a scary
night'),nl,
  write('and when you get the Nani it''s not
going'),nl,
  write('to smell right.'),nl,nl.

% The help command

nshelp:-
  write('Use simple English sentences to enter
commands.'),nl,
  write('The commands can cause you to:'),nl,
  nl,
  write('    go to a room           (ex. go to the
office)'),nl,
  write('    look around            (ex. look)'),nl,
  write('    look in something      (ex. look in the
desk)'),nl,
  write('    take something         (ex. take the
apple)'),nl,
  write('    drop something         (ex. drop the
apple)'),nl,
```

```
  write('   eat something           (ex. eat the
apple)'),nl,
  write('   turn something on        (ex. turn on the
light)'),nl,
  write('   inventory your things (ex.
inventory)'),nl,
  nl,
  write('The examples are verbose, terser commands
and synonyms'),nl,
  write('are usually accepted.'),nl,nl,
  write('Hit any key to continue.'),nl,
  get0(_),
  look.

hint:-
  write('You need to get to the cellar, and you
can''t unless'),nl,
  write('you get some light. You can''t turn on the
cellar'),nl,
  write('light, but there is a flash light in the
desk in the'),nl,
  write('office you might use.'),nl,nl,
  look.

% Initial facts describing the world.  Rooms and
doors do not change,
% so they are compiled.

room(office).
room(kitchen).
room('dining room').
room(hall).
room(cellar).

door(office,hall).
door(hall,'dining room').
door('dining room',kitchen).
door(kitchen,cellar).
door(kitchen,office).

connect(X,Y):-
  door(X,Y).
connect(X,Y):-
  door(Y,X).
```

```
% These facts are all subject to change during the
game, so rather
% than being compiled, they are "asserted" to the
listener at
% run time.  This predicate is called when "nanisrch"
starts up.

init_dynamic_facts:-
  assertz(location(desk,office)),
  assertz(location(apple,kitchen)),
  assertz(location(flashlight,desk)),
  assertz(location('washing machine',cellar)),
  assertz(location(nani,'washing machine')),
  assertz(location(table,kitchen)),
  assertz(location(crackers,desk)),
  assertz(location(broccoli,kitchen)),
  assertz(here(kitchen)),
  assertz(turned_off(flashlight)).

furniture(desk).
furniture('washing machine').
furniture(table).

edible(apple).
edible(crackers).

tastes_yuchy(broccoli).

%%%%%%%% COMMANDS %%%%%%%%%%%%%%%%%%%%%%%%%%%%%%%%

% goto moves the player from room to room.

goto(Room):-
  can_go(Room),                    % check for legal
move
  puzzle(goto(Room)),              % check for special
conditions
  moveto(Room),                    % go there and tell
the player
  look.
goto(_):- look.

can_go(Room):-                     % if there is a
connection it
  here(Here),                      % is a legal move.
```

```
   connect(Here,Room),!.
can_go(Room):-
   respond(['You can''t get to ',Room,' from
here']),fail.

moveto(Room):-                        % update the database
with the
   retract(here(_)),                  % new room
   asserta(here(Room)).

% look lists the things in a room, and the
connections

look:-
   here(Here),
   respond(['You are in the ',Here]),
   write('You can see the following things:'),nl,
   list_things(Here),
   write('You can go to the following rooms:'),nl,
   list_connections(Here).

list_things(Place):-
   location(X,Place),
   tab(2),write(X),nl,
   fail.
list_things(_).

list_connections(Place):-
   connect(Place,X),
   tab(2),write(X),nl,
   fail.
list_connections(_).

% look_in allows the player to look inside a thing
which might
% contain other things

look_in(Thing):-
   location(_,Thing),                 % make sure
there's at least one
   write('The '),write(Thing),write(' contains:'),nl,
   list_things(Thing).
look_in(Thing):-
   respond(['There is nothing in the ',Thing]).
```

% take allows the player to take something. As long as the thing is
% contained in the room it can be taken, even if the adventurer hasn't
% looked in the the container which contains it. Also the thing
% must not be furniture.

```
take(Thing):-
  is_here(Thing),
  is_takable(Thing),
  move(Thing,have),
  respond(['You now have the ',Thing]).

is_here(Thing):-
  here(Here),
  contains(Thing,Here),!.          % don't backtrack
is_here(Thing):-
  respond(['There is no ',Thing,' here']),
  fail.

contains(Thing,Here):-             % recursive
definition to find
  location(Thing,Here).            % things contained
in things etc.
contains(Thing,Here):-
  location(Thing,X),
  contains(X,Here).

is_takable(Thing):-                % you can't take
the furniture
  furniture(Thing),
  respond(['You can''t pick up a ',Thing]),
  !,fail.
is_takable(_).                     % not furniture,
ok to take

move(Thing,have):-
  retract(location(Thing,_)),      % take it from its
old place
  asserta(have(Thing)).            % and add to your
possessions
```

% drop - allows the player to transfer a possession to a room

```
drop(Thing):-
  have(Thing),                        % you must have
the thing to drop it
  here(Here),                         % where are we
  retract(have(Thing)),
  asserta(location(Thing,Here)).
drop(Thing):-
  respond(['You don''t have the ',Thing]).

% eat, because every adventure game lets you eat
stuff.

eat(Thing):-
  have(Thing),
  eat2(Thing).
eat(Thing):-
  respond(['You don''t have the ',Thing]).

eat2(Thing):-
  edible(Thing),
  retract(have(Thing)),
  respond(['That ',Thing,' was good']).
eat2(Thing):-
  tastes_yuchy(Thing),
  respond(['Three year olds don''t eat ',Thing]).
eat2(Thing):-
  respond(['You can''t eat a ',Thing]).

% inventory list your possesions

inventory:-
  have(X),                            % make sure you
have at least one thing
  write('You have: '),nl,
  list_possessions.
inventory:-
  write('You have nothing'),nl.

list_possessions:-
  have(X),
  tab(2),write(X),nl,
  fail.
list_possessions.
```

```
% turn_on recognizes two cases.  If the player tries
to simply turn
% on the light, it is assumed this is the room light,
and the
% appropriate error message is issued.  Otherwise
turn_on has to
% refer to an object which is turned_off.

turn_on(light):-
  respond(['You can''t reach the switch and there''s
nothing to stand on']).
turn_on(Thing):-
  have(Thing),
  turn_on2(Thing).
turn_on(Thing):-
  respond(['You don''t have the ',Thing]).

turn_on2(Thing):-
  turned_on(Thing),
  respond([Thing,' is already on']).
turn_on2(Thing):-
  turned_off(Thing),
  retract(turned_off(Thing)),
  asserta(turned_on(Thing)),
  respond([Thing,' turned on']).
turn_on2(Thing):-
  respond(['You can''t turn a ',Thing,' on']).

% turn_off - I didn't feel like implementing turn_off

turn_off(Thing):-
  respond(['I lied about being able to turn things
off']).

% The only special puzzle in Nani Search has to do
with going to the
% cellar.  Puzzle is only called from goto for this
reason.  Other
% puzzles pertaining to other commands could easily
be added.

puzzle(goto(cellar)):-
  have(flashlight),
  turned_on(flashlight),!.
puzzle(goto(cellar)):-
```

```
  write('You can''t go to the cellar because it''s
dark in the'),nl,
  write('cellar, and you''re afraid of the
dark.'),nl,
  !,fail.
puzzle(_).
```

% respond simplifies writing a mixture of literals
and variables

```
respond([]):-
  write('.'),nl,nl.
respond([H|T]):-
  write(H),
  respond(T).
```

% Simple English command listener. It does some
semantic checking
% and allows for various synonyms. Within a
restricted subset of
% English, a command can be phrased many ways. Also
non grammatical
% constructs are understood, for example just giving
a room name
% is interpreted as the command to goto that room.

% Some interpretation is based on the situation.
Notice that when
% the player says turn on the light it is ambiguous.
It could mean
% the room light (which can't be turned on in the
game) or the
% flash light. If the player has the flash light it
is interpreted
% as flash light, otherwise it is interpreted as room
light.

```
get_command(C):-
  readlist(L),        % reads a sentence and puts
[it,in,list,form]
  command(X,L,[]),    % call the grammar for command
  C =.. X,!.          % make the command list a
structure
get_command(_):-
  respond(['I don''t understand, try again or type
```

```
help']),fail.

% The grammar doesn't have to be real English.  There
are two
% types of commands in Nani Search, those with and
without a
% single argument.  A special case is also made for
the command
% goto which can be activated by simply giving a room
name.

command([Pred,Arg]) -->
verb(Type,Pred),nounphrase(Type,Arg).
command([Pred]) --> verb(intran,Pred).
command([goto,Arg]) --> noun(go_place,Arg).

% Recognize three types of verbs.  Each verb
corresponds to a command,
% but there are many synonyms allowed.  For example
the command
% turn_on will be triggered by either "turn on" or
"switch on".

verb(go_place,goto) --> go_verb.
verb(thing,V) --> tran_verb(V).
verb(intran,V) --> intran_verb(V).

go_verb --> [go].
go_verb --> [go,to].
go_verb --> [g].

tran_verb(take) --> [take].
tran_verb(take) --> [pick,up].
tran_verb(drop) --> [drop].
tran_verb(drop) --> [put].
tran_verb(drop) --> [put,down].
tran_verb(eat) --> [eat].
tran_verb(turn_on) --> [turn,on].
tran_verb(turn_on) --> [switch,on].
tran_verb(turn_off) --> [turn,off].
tran_verb(look_in) --> [look,in].
tran_verb(look_in) --> [look].
tran_verb(look_in) --> [open].

intran_verb(inventory) --> [inventory].
```

```
intran_verb(inventory) --> [i].
intran_verb(look) --> [look].
intran_verb(look) --> [look,around].
intran_verb(look) --> [l].
intran_verb(quit) --> [quit].
intran_verb(quit) --> [exit].
intran_verb(quit) --> [end].
intran_verb(quit) --> [bye].
intran_verb(nshelp) --> [help].
intran_verb(hint) --> [hint].
```

```
% a noun phrase is just a noun with an optional
determiner in front.
```

```
nounphrase(Type,Noun) --> det,noun(Type,Noun).
nounphrase(Type,Noun) --> noun(Type,Noun).
```

```
det --> [the].
det --> [a].
```

```
% Nouns are defined as rooms, or things located
somewhere.  We define
% special cases for those things represented in Nani
Search by two
% words.  We can't expect the user to type the name
in quotes.
```

```
noun(go_place,R) --> [R], {room(R)}.
noun(go_place,'dining room') --> [dining,room].
```

```
noun(thing,T) --> [T], {location(T,_)}.
noun(thing,T) --> [T], {have(T)}.
noun(thing,flashlight) --> [flash,light].
noun(thing,'washing machine') --> [washing,machine].
noun(thing,'dirty clothes') --> [dirty,clothes].
```

```
% If the player has just typed light, it can be
interpreted three ways.
% If a room name is before it, it must be a room
light.  If the
% player has the flash light, assume it means the
flash light.  Otherwise
% assume it is the room light.
```

```
noun(thing,light) --> [X,light], {room(X)}.
```

```
noun(thing,flashlight) --> [light],
{have(flashlight)}.
noun(thing,light) --> [light].

% readlist - read a list of words, based on a
Clocksin & Mellish
% example.

readlist(L):-
  write('> '),
  read_word_list(L).

read_word_list([W|Ws]) :-
  get0(C),
  readword(C, W, C1),        % Read word starting with
C, C1 is first new
  restsent(C1, Ws), !.       % character - use it to
get rest of sentence

restsent(C,[]) :- lastword(C), !. % Nothing left if
hit last-word marker
restsent(C,[W1|Ws]) :-
  readword(C,W1,C1),         % Else read next word and
rest of sentence
  restsent(C1,Ws).

readword(C,W,C1) :-          % Some words are single
characters
  single_char(C),            % i.e. punctuation
  !,
  name(W, [C]),              % get as an atom
  get0(C1).
readword(C, W, C1) :-
  is_num(C),                 % if we have a number --
  !,
  number_word(C, W, C1, _).  % convert it to a genuine
number
readword(C,W,C2) :-          % otherwise if character
does not
  in_word(C, NewC),          % delineate end of word -
keep
  get0(C1),                  % accumulating them until
  restword(C1,Cs,C2),        % we have all the word
  name(W, [NewC|Cs]).        % then make it an atom
readword(C,W,C2) :-          % otherwise
```

```
    get0(C1),
    readword(C1,W,C2).        % start a new word


restword(C, [NewC|Cs], C2) :-
    in_word(C, NewC),
    get0(C1),
    restword(C1, Cs, C2).
restword(C, [], C).



single_char(`,).
single_char(`;).
single_char(`:).
single_char(`?).
single_char(`!).
single_char(`.).



in_word(C, C) :- C >= `a, C =< `z.
in_word(C, L) :- C >= `A, C =< `Z, L is C + 32.
in_word(`',`').
in_word(`-,`-).
```

% Have character C (known integer) - keep reading
integers and build
% up the number until we hit a non-integer. Return
this in C1,
% and return the computed number in W.

```
number_word(C, W, C1, Pow10) :-
    is_num(C),
    !,
    get0(C2),
    number_word(C2, W1, C1, P10),
    Pow10 is P10 * 10,
    W is integer(((C - `0) * Pow10) + W1).
number_word(C, 0, C, 0.1).



is_num(C) :-
    C =< `9,
    C >= `0.
```

% These symbols delineate end of sentence

```
lastword(10).    % end if new line entered
lastword(`.).
lastword(`!).
lastword(`?).
```

Family

```
% GENE.PRO - genealogical relationships
%
%
% A Prolog database of relations derived from basic
information about
% individuals.  The relations ships can all be read
as 'relationship
% of', so for example, parent(P,C) means P is parent
of C.
%
% When there is a performance trade-of in the
implementation of a rule,
% it is assumed that in general the second argument
of a relation will
% most likely be bound.  See for example
full_sibling/2, which will
% have a smaller search for full_sibling(X,joe), than
full_sibling(joe,X).
%
% This code is used as an example of an embedded
Prolog application
% in both the directories APISAMP\WGENE and
APISAMP\WGENEVB.
% One is a C++ application and the other Visual
Basic.
%
% To use this code from Prolog, consult it in the
listener and use the
% following predicates:
%
% open(F) - opens a file of family relationships, ex.
open('england.fam').
%     open/1 just does a consult, so you can use
consult instead.
% close - retracts all the persons currently defined
% save(F) - saves the persons in the named file
% add_person(Name, Mother, Father, Gender, Spouse) -
adds a person
%     fact with the specified attributes, checking
semantics as it does
% Relationship(P1, P2) - any relationship query, such
as child(X,Y).
```

```
% relation(R, P1, P2) - can be used to find the
relationship between
%      individuals as well as pose relationship
queries.

parent(P,C) :-
 (mother(P,C) ; father(P,C)).

child(C,P) :- parent(P,C).

son(C,P) :- parent(P,C), male(C).

daughter(C,P) :- parent(P,C), female(C).

wife(W,P) :-
  spouse(W,P),
  female(W).

husband(H,P) :-
  spouse(H,P),
  male(H).

ancestor(A,P) :-
  parent(A,P).
ancestor(A,P) :-
  parent(X,P),
  ancestor(A,X).

descendent(D,P) :-
  parent(P,D).
descendent(D,P) :-
  parent(P,X),
  descendent(D,X).

full_sibling(S1, S2) :-
  mother(M,S2),
  mother(M,S1),
  S1 \= S2,
  father(F,S1),
  father(F,S2).

half_sibling(S1, S2) :-
  mother(M,S2),
  mother(M,S1),
  S1 \= S2,
```

```
    father(F1,S1),
    father(F2,S2),
    F1 \= F2.
half_sibling(S1, S2) :-
    father(F,S2),
    father(F,S1),
    S1 \= S2,
    mother(M1,S1),
    mother(M2,S2),
    M1 \= M2.

sibling(S1, S2) :-
    full_sibling(S1,S2).
sibling(S1, S2) :-
    half_sibling(S1,S2).

sister(S,P) :-
    sibling(S,P),
    female(S).

brother(B,P) :-
    sibling(B,P),
    male(B).

step_sibling(S1, S2) :-
    parent(P2, S2),
    spouse(M2, P2),
    parent(M2, S1),
    not(parent(M2,S2)),
    not(half_sibling(S1,S2)).

uncle(U,X) :-
    parent(P,X),
    brother(U,P).

aunt(A,X) :-
    parent(P,X),
    sister(A,P).

step_parent(P2,C) :-
    parent(P,C),
    spouse(P2,P),
    not(parent(P2,C)).

step_mother(M,C) :- step_parent(M,C), female(M).
```

```
step_father(F,C) :- step_parent(F,C), male(F).

step_child(C2,P) :- step_parent(P,C2).

step_daughter(D,P) :- step_child(D,P), female(D).

step_son(S,P) :- step_child(S,P), male(S).

nephew(N,X) :-
  sibling(S,X),
  parent(S,N),
  male(N).

niece(N,X) :-
  sibling(S,X),
  parent(S,N),
  female(N).

cousin(X,Y) :-
  parent(P,Y),
  sibling(S,P),
  parent(S,X).

grandmother(GM,X) :-
  parent(P,X),
  mother(GM,P).

grandfather(GF,X) :-
  parent(P,X),
  father(GF,P).

grandparent(GP,X) :-
  parent(P,X),
  parent(GP,P).

grandson(GS,X) :-
  grandchild(GS,X),
  male(GS).

granddaughter(GD,X) :-
  grandchild(GD,X),
  female(GD).

grandchild(GC,X) :-
```

```
  parent(X,C),
  parent(C,GC).


%-------------------------------------------------------
-------------------
% relation/3 - used to find relationships between
individuals
%

relations([parent, wife, husband, ancestor,
descendent, full_sibling,
    half_sibling, sibling, sister, brother,
step_sibling, uncle,
    aunt, mother, father, child, son, daughter,
step_parent,
    step_child, step_mother, step_father, step_son,
step_daughter,
    nephew, niece, cousin, grandmother, grandfather,
grandparent,
    grandson, granddaughter, grandchild]).

relation(R, X, Y) :-
  relations(Rs),
  member(R,Rs),
  Q =.. [R,X,Y],
  call(Q).


%-------------------------------------------------------
-------------------
% person object
%
% These predicates define the interface to a person.
All of the
% genealogical rules are based on these predicates,
which are
% based on the basic representation of a person.
These are the
% only rules which need to be changed if the
representation of
% a person is changed.
%
% The current representation is flat database
relations of the form:
%    person(Name, Gender, Mother, Father, Spouse).
```

```
%

add(Name,Gender,Mother,Father,Spouse) :-
  assert(person(Name,Gender,Mother,Father,Spouse)).
add(Name,_,_,_,_) :-
  delete(Name),
  fail.

open(FileName) :-
  consult(FileName).

close :-
  retractall(person(_,_,_,_,_)).

save(FileName) :-
  tell(FileName),
  listing(person),
  told.

delete(X) :-
  retract(person(X,_,_,_,_)).

person(X) :-
  person(X,_,_,_,_).

male(X) :-
  person(X,male,_,_,_).

female(Y) :-
  person(Y,female,_,_,_).

mother(M,C) :-
  person(C,_,M,_,_).

father(F,C) :-
  person(C,_,_,F,_).

spouse(S,P) :-
  person(P,_,_,_,S),
  S \= single.

%----------------------------------------------------
------------------
% Semantic Integrity Checks on Update
%
```

```
add_person(Name,Gender,Mother,Father,Spouse) :-
  retractall(message(_)),
  dup_check(Name),
  add(Name,Gender,Mother,Father,Spouse),
  ancestor_check(Name),
  mother_check(Name, Gender, Mother),
  father_check(Name, Gender, Father),
  spouse_check(Name, Spouse).

dup_check(Name) :-
  person(Name),
  assert(message($Person is already in database$)),
  !, fail.
dup_check(_).

ancestor_check(Name) :-
  ancestor(Name,Name),
  assert(message($Person is their own ancestor/
descendent$)),
  !, fail.
ancestor_check(_).

mother_check(_, _, Mother) :- not(person(Mother)), !.
mother_check(_, _, Mother) :-
  male(Mother),
  assert(message($Person's mother is a man$)),
  !, fail.
mother_check(Name, male, _) :-
  mother(Name, X),
  assert(message($Person, a male, is someone's
mother$)),
  !, fail.
mother_check(_,_,_).

father_check(_, _, Father) :- not(person(Father)), !.
father_check(_, _, Father) :-
  female(Father),
  assert(message($Person's father is a man$)),
  !, fail.
father_check(Name, female, _) :-
  father(Name, X),
  assert(message($Person, a female, is someone's
father$)),
  !, fail.
```

```
father_check(_,_,_).

spouse_check(Name, Spouse) :-
  spouse(Name, X),
  X \= Spouse,
  assert(message($Person is already someone else's
spouse$)),
  !, fail.
spouse_check(Name, Spouse) :-
  blood_relative(Name, Spouse),
  assert(message($Person is a blood relative of
spouse$)),
  !, fail.
spouse_check(_,_).

blood_relative(X,Y) :- (ancestor(X,Y);
ancestor(Y,X)).
blood_relative(X,Y) :- sibling(X,Y).
blood_relative(X,Y) :- cousin(X,Y).
blood_relative(X,Y) :- (uncle(X,Y); uncle(Y,X)).
blood_relative(X,Y) :- (aunt(X,Y); aunt(Y,X)).
```

Custord

```
% CUSTORD


% This is a sample Prolog program which implements a
portion
% of a customer order inventory application.  It is
not intended to
% be complete, and only illustrates the concept of
writing a database
% application in Prolog.

% This example extends the concept of an intelligent
database to include
% a full database application.  It is really a rule
based approach to
% transaction processing.  In fact a large percentage
of the procedural
% code normally written in database applications has
to do with
% enforcing semantic integrity rules involving
multiple records.

% The distinction between data and process is
thoroughly blurred.  Both
% reside together in the same database.

% There is pure data as it might be defined in a
relational database
% (customer, item, inventory, order); there are rules
which really
% represent data views (item_quant); there are rules
which add
% intelligence to the database (good_customer,
valid_order); and there
% are rules which are processes (order,
report_inventory).

main :- order.

% customer(Name, Town, Credit-rating).

customer(dennis, winchester, xxx).
```

```
customer(dave, lexington, aaa).
customer(ron, lexington, bbb).
customer(julie, winchester, aaa).
customer(jawaid, cambridge, aaa).
customer(tom, newton, ccc).


% item(Number, Name, Reorder-quantity).

item(p1,thing,10).
item(p2,stuff,10).
item(p3,article,10).
item(p4,object,10).
item(p5,substance,10).
item(p6,piece,10).
item(p7,matter,10).

% inventory(Number, Quantity).

inventory(p1,10).
inventory(p2,10).
inventory(p3,10).
inventory(p4,78).
inventory(p5,23).
inventory(p6,14).
inventory(p7,8).

% item-inv view or join

item_quant(Item, Quantity):-
  item(Partno, Item, _),
  inventory(Partno, Quantity).

% reorder if inventory below reorder point

reorder(Item):-
  item(Partno, Item, Reorder_point),
  inventory(Partno, Quantity),
  Quantity < Reorder_point,
  write('Time to reorder '),
  write(Item), nl.
reorder(Item):-
  write('Inventory level ok for '),
  write(Item), nl.

% a good customer has a credit rating of aaa
```

```
% or lives in winchester
% or has ordered something

good_customer(Cust):-
  customer(Cust, _, aaa).
good_customer(Cust):-
  customer(Cust, winchester, _).
good_customer(Cust):-
  order(Cust, _, _).

% process order

order:-
  write('Customer: '),
  read(Customer),
  write('Item: '),
  read(Item),
  write('Quantity: '),
  read(Quantity),
  valid_order(Customer,Item,Quantity),
  asserta(order(Customer,Item,Quantity)),
  update_inventory(Item,Quantity),
  reorder(Item).

% an order is valid if
% it doesn't go below zero inventory and
% the customer is a good customer

valid_order(C, I, Q):-
  item(Partno, I, _),
  inventory(Partno, Onhand),
  Q =< Onhand,
  good_customer(C).
valid_order(C, I, Q):-
  write('Bad order'),
  nl,
  fail.

% update the inventory

update_inventory(I,Q):-
  item(Pn, I, _),
  inventory(Pn, Amount),
  NewQ is Amount - Q,
  retract(inventory(Pn, Amount)),
```

```
  asserta(inventory(Pn, NewQ)).

% inventory report

report_inventory:-
  item_quant(I, Q),
  write(I), tab(1),
  write(Q), nl,
  fail.
report_inventory:-true.
```

Birds

```
% BIRDS
```

```
% This is a sample of a classification expert system
for identification
% of certain kinds of birds.  The rules are rough
excerpts from "Birds of
% North America" by Robbins, Bruum, Zim, and Singer.

% This type of expert system can easily use Prolog's
built in inferencing
% system.  While trying to satisfy the goal "bird" it
tries to satisfy
% various subgoals, some of which will ask for
information from the
% user.

% The information is all stored as attribute-value
pairs.  The attribute
% is represented as a predicate, and the value as the
argument to the
% predicate.  For example, the attribute-value pair
"color-brown" is
% stored "color(brown)".

% "identify" is the high level goal that starts the
program.  The
% predicate "known/3" is used to remember answers to
questions, so it
% is cleared at the beginning of the run.

% The rules of identification are the bulk of the
code.  They break up
% the problem into identifying orders and families
before identifying
% the actual birds.

% The end of the code lists those attribute-value
pairs which need
% to be asked for, and defines the predicate "ask"
and "menuask"
% which are used to get information from the user,
```

and remember it.

```
main :- identify.

identify:-
  retractall(known(_,_,_)),    % clear stored
information
  bird(X),
  write('The bird is a '),write(X),nl.
identify:-
  write('I can''t identify that bird'),nl.

order(tubenose):-
  nostrils(external_tubular),
  live(at_sea),
  bill(hooked).
order(waterfowl):-
  feet(webbed),
  bill(flat).
order(falconiforms):-
  eats(meat),
  feet(curved_talons),
  bill(sharp_hooked).
order(passerformes):-
  feet(one_long_backward_toe).

family(albatross):-
  order(tubenose),
  size(large),
  wings(long_narrow).
family(swan):-
  order(waterfowl),
  neck(long),
  color(white),
  flight(ponderous).
family(goose):-
  order(waterfowl),
  size(plump),
  flight(powerful).
family(duck):-
  order(waterfowl),
  feed(on_water_surface),
  flight(agile).
family(vulture):-
  order(falconiforms),
```

```
    feed(scavange),
    wings(broad).
  family(falcon):-
    order(falconiforms),
    wings(long_pointed),
    head(large),
    tail(narrow_at_tip).
  family(flycatcher):-
    order(passerformes),
    bill(flat),
    eats(flying_insects).
  family(swallow):-
    order(passerformes),
    wings(long_pointed),
    tail(forked),
    bill(short).

  bird(laysan_albatross):-
    family(albatross),
    color(white).
  bird(black_footed_albatross):-
    family(albatross),
    color(dark).
  bird(fulmar):-
    order(tubenose),
    size(medium),
    flight(flap_glide).
  bird(whistling_swan):-
    family(swan),
    voice(muffled_musical_whistle).
  bird(trumpeter_swan):-
    family(swan),
    voice(loud_trumpeting).
  bird(canada_goose):-
    family(goose),
    season(winter),                    % rules can be
further broken down
    country(united_states),            % to include regions
and migration
    head(black),                       % patterns
    cheek(white).
  bird(canada_goose):-
    family(goose),
    season(summer),
    country(canada),
```

```
  head(black),
  cheek(white).
bird(snow_goose):-
  family(goose),
  color(white).
bird(mallard):-
  family(duck),                    % different rules
for male
  voice(quack),
  head(green).
bird(mallard):-
  family(duck),                    % and female
  voice(quack),
  color(mottled_brown).
bird(pintail):-
  family(duck),
  voice(short_whistle).
bird(turkey_vulture):-
  family(vulture),
  flight_profile(v_shaped).
bird(california_condor):-
  family(vulture),
  flight_profile(flat).
bird(sparrow_hawk):-
  family(falcon),
  eats(insects).
bird(peregrine_falcon):-
  family(falcon),
  eats(birds).
bird(great_crested_flycatcher):-
  family(flycatcher),
  tail(long_rusty).
bird(ash_throated_flycatcher):-
  family(flycatcher),
  throat(white).
bird(barn_swallow):-
  family(swallow),
  tail(forked).
bird(cliff_swallow):-
  family(swallow),
  tail(square).
bird(purple_martin):-
  family(swallow),
  color(dark).
```

```
country(united_states):- region(new_england).
country(united_states):- region(south_east).
country(united_states):- region(mid_west).
country(united_states):- region(south_west).
country(united_states):- region(north_west).
country(united_states):- region(mid_atlantic).


country(canada):- province(ontario).
country(canada):- province(quebec).
country(canada):- province(etc).


region(new_england):-
  state(X),
  member(X, [massachusetts, vermont, etc]).
region(south_east):-
  state(X),
  member(X, [florida, mississippi, etc]).


region(canada):-
  province(X),
  member(X, [ontario,quebec,etc]).


nostrils(X):- ask(nostrils,X).
live(X):- ask(live,X).
bill(X):- ask(bill,X).
size(X):- menuask(size,X,[large,plump,medium,small]).
eats(X):- ask(eats,X).
feet(X):- ask(feet,X).
wings(X):- ask(wings,X).
neck(X):- ask(neck,X).
color(X):- ask(color,X).
flight(X):- menuask(flight,X,
[ponderous,powerful,agile,flap_glide,other]).
feed(X):- ask(feed,X).
head(X):- ask(head,X).
tail(X):- menuask(tail,X,
[narrow_at_tip,forked,long_rusty,square,other]).
voice(X):- ask(voice,X).
season(X):- menuask(season,X,[winter,summer]).
cheek(X):- ask(cheek,X).
flight_profile(X):- menuask(flight_profile,X,
[flat,v_shaped,other]).
throat(X):- ask(throat,X).
state(X):- menuask(state,X,
[massachusetts,vermont,florida,mississippi,etc]).
```

```
province(X):- menuask(province,X,
[ontario,quebec,etc]).

% "ask" is responsible for getting information from
the user, and remembering
% the users response.  If it doesn't already know the
answer to a question
% it will ask the user.  It then asserts the answer.
It recognizes two
% cases of knowledge: 1) the attribute-value is known
to be true,
%                     2) the attribute-value is known
to be false.

% This means an attribute might have multiple values.
A third test to
% see if the attribute has another value could be
used to enforce
% single valued attributes. (This test is commented
out below)

% For this system the menuask is used for attributes
which are single
% valued

% "ask" only deals with simple yes or no answers.  a
"yes" is the only
% yes value.  any other response is considered a
"no".

ask(Attribute,Value):-
   known(yes,Attribute,Value),    % succeed if we
know its true
   !.                             % and dont look any
further
ask(Attribute,Value):-
   known(_,Attribute,Value),      % fail if we know
its false
   !, fail.

% ask(Attribute,_):-
%    known(yes,Attribute,_),      % fail if we know
its some other value.
%    !, fail.                     % the cut in clause
#1 ensures that if
```

```
                                   % we get here the
value is wrong.
ask(A,V):-
  write(A:V),                      % if we get here,
we need to ask.
  write('? (yes or no): '),
  read(Y),                         % get the answer
  asserta(known(Y,A,V)),           % remember it so we
dont ask again.
  Y = yes.                         % succeed or fail
based on answer.


% "menuask" is like ask, only it gives the user a
menu to to choose
% from rather than a yes on no answer.  In this case
there is no
% need to check for a negative since "menuask"
ensures there will
% be some positive answer.

menuask(Attribute,Value,_):-
  known(yes,Attribute,Value),      % succeed if we
know
  !.
menuask(Attribute,_,_):-
  known(yes,Attribute,_),          % fail if its some
other value
  !, fail.


menuask(Attribute,AskValue,Menu):-
  nl,write('What is the value for
'),write(Attribute),write('?'),nl,
  display_menu(Menu),
  write('Enter the number of choice> '),
  read(Num),nl,
  pick_menu(Num,AnswerValue,Menu),
  asserta(known(yes,Attribute,AnswerValue)),
  AskValue = AnswerValue.          % succeed or
fail based on answer

display_menu(Menu):-
  disp_menu(1,Menu), !.            % make sure we
fail on backtracking


disp_menu(_,[]).
```

```
disp_menu(N,[Item | Rest]):-              % recursively
write the head of
   write(N),write(' : '),write(Item),nl, % the list
and disp_menu the tail
   NN is N + 1,
   disp_menu(NN,Rest).


pick_menu(N,Val,Menu):-
   integer(N),                            % make sure they
gave a number
   pic_menu(1,N,Val,Menu), !.             % start at one
pick_menu(Val,Val,_).                     % if they didn't
enter a number, use

                                          % what they
entered as the value


pic_menu(_,_,none_of_the_above,[]).       % if we've
exhausted the list
pic_menu(N,N, Item, [Item|_]).            % the counter
matches the number
pic_menu(Ctr,N, Val, [_|Rest]):-
   NextCtr is Ctr + 1,                    % try the next
one
   pic_menu(NextCtr, N, Val, Rest).
```

Made in the USA
Coppell, TX
25 February 2020